BURY MY CHILDREN
IN A STRANGE LAND

by
C.W. Cissna

ISBN-13: 978-1469920078
ISBN-10: 1469920077

Privately Published
Albuquerque, NM
bcissna@aol.com

THIRD EDITION
2021
2017
2012
2023

"If you teach them where they come from, they won't need as much help finding where they are going!"
Cordelia Carothers "Aunt Dee" Geoghegan
(1894-1987)

Books for Researchers
Available at Amazon.com

House of Cessna, Book One: In 1903, Howard Cessna began to unravel 1000 years of history for this great family. He introduced his first journal at grand family reunion held in 1904 at the World's Fair in St. Louis. This book began a passionate search by the family's historians to learn the heartbeat of our ancestry. It is no longer in print, but it is copied here as a place to begin your journey.

House of Cessna, Book Two: Howard Cessna's work "House of Cessna, Second Series" published in 1935, is reprinted here. Some newer information is included.

House of Cessna, Book Three: A report of research done in France. Research there is far from complete. The history of the family in France remains cloudy, with the earliest reference to the name hinting to the 1065 army of William the Conqueror. Book III provides clues to ancestral secrets of Castles and Coats of Arms.

Early Cessna Farms: Ancient cartographic records and time faded land deeds chronicle the blood soaked soil of our family's farmsteads, bravely established during the years from 1720-1820. They created homes and businesses while facing nine different wars with native peoples. These documents bear witness to the relentless toil and unyielding determination that carved our lineage into the very earth itself. Our family's footsteps are etched upon the maps, like scars of triumph and resilience.

Our Cessna Legacy: Among the most mesmerizing of ancestors is Major John Cessna, patriarch of the majority of branches on our family tree. Farmer, teamster, soldier, sheriff, politician, legislator, veteran of three wars, and Commanding Officer during the American Revolution; John Cessna epitomizes the courage and tenacity of this great family. His life is presented here in the framework of 383 factual references, quotes, and maps. This is your opportunity to meet one of the most paramount patriarchs of the family.

Reconstructed Census: Our American Experience began with two brothers who landed in New Castle, Delaware in 1718. In less than 100 years the family had established itself in nine states. This volume unveils every move west by our forefathers. It is revised as new information is discovered.

Muster Call: This family has a long history of heroes answering the call to protect our neighbors and county. Here is an Honor Roll of those men and women who served to defend freedom and democracy for the past 300 years. Where possible, their place on the family tree and a description of their service is provided. It is incomplete because every month a new member of our family steps forward to serve.

Our Fifteen Minutes: This album of news clippings recounts a wide variety of family exploits. Some are humorous, and some are sad. All reveal unique qualities of this great clan.

Tri-Centennial Celebration and Cessna Reunion. To celebrate the 300th anniversary of the Cessna brothers landing in America, a National Reunion was held in Bedford, PA in 2018. Here is the week of activities and a guide to visiting dozens of historical family locations for those making new pilgrimages.

Cessnas Gather: Following the overwhelming success of the National Reunion of 2018 in Bedford, PA, a keepsake album was published. It also contains exciting new data which was brought by researchers who came from across our nation.

Those Who Rest at Woods Cemetery, Rainsburg, PA: No church yard anywhere holds more members of this family. In celebration of the family's 300th Anniversary, Jerry Cessna completed a survey of grave inscriptions and matched them with obituaries from local newspapers.

OUR AMERICA SERIES:
A history of America through
fictionalized accounts of the lives of family member
Available at Amazon.com

Bury My Children in a Strange Land. After fleeing his home in France under persecution for his religion, enduring five frustrating years of soldiering, and surviving 20 miserable years of trying to farm the truculent soil of Northern Ireland, boarded an aging and fragile ship bound for a promise of freedom. In 1718, he and two sons made an epic and heartbreaking journey to Pennsylvania's wilderness.

The Reluctant American. Captured by Ottawa at age ten, and raised for five years to be a warrior, Joseph Cessna escaped in 1761 to a world which had changed greatly. During the Revolution his warrior skills protected his neighbors. Following the war, he became a founding father of the Michigan Territory. Throughout his life he was deeply uncertain if he was French, English, Ottawa, or American. In the end, he proved to be the essence of every American.

Forgotten Courage. Like so many young men, the excitement of fighting the oppressive English Army kindled a patriotic flame in the heart of Stephen Cessna. Orphaned at age 5, the now 19-year-old frontier sharpshooter was among the first to volunteer in General Washington's Continental Army.

Let Me Live in Peace. Ending English Rule in the colonies opened a vicious competition for power among the new Americans. Colonel Charles Cessna had served valiantly in defense of the Pennsylvania Frontier throughout the revolution. Honorably he served in state and local government. Legal machinations and rivalries made during the war branded him as a pariah. This exiled him to a 25-year search for peace in three different frontier states.

Tomahawks and Teacups. At the tender age of 7, Jonathan was taken from his family by Ottawa warriors. For five years he lived the tortured life of a slave. Once free, a burning hatred for his captors led him on a convoluted path of joy and pain. It ended with his death fighting at the side of Col. Daniel Boone. He rests in a hidden grave near Piqua, Ohio which has long been forgotten even though it was his blood which purchased freedom for those families who currently live there.

Will This Country Survive? In her second war with England, the American Experiment nearly came to a sudden and violent end. Only the sacrifices of the bravest and most tenacious citizen-warriors would save it from destruction. Members of our family offered their lives to preserve this country. Their stories are recorded for the ages in this colorful collection

Where Can We Prosper? In the second half-century of America's history, people were constantly buffeted by violent storms from disease, weather, politics, and financial catastrophes. Among the courageous souls who moved this country westward was Samuel Cissna. He invested his strength and life by clinging tenaciously to his dream of a better life for his children. The power of his determination still courses through the blood of his descendants.

A Nation and Family Divided. It was called the war for America's Soul. It pitted brother against brother, cousin against cousin, and father against son. Defending the ideals of their faith, and loyalty to their community, 84 members of this family took up arms against each other. The experiences of this one family mirrored the pain and anguish of the entire country. Their stories are heartbreakingly true.

Civilizing a Pioneer Generation. It is known as the Wild West, and it fed the soil of this beautiful land with the life blood of both the good and the bad. Sheriff George Sisney stood bravely in the face of the deadliest family feud in America's history. He was murdered for his courage. Colonel James Cisney was drafted by the President to manage relations with tribal nations. His service carried him to the killing field known as Wounded Knee, and to the greed filled madness of the Oklahoma Land Rush. The stories of these two men unmask the determination required to tame the west.

INTRODUCTION

In 1690, Louis XIV, King of France repealed the Edict of Nantes. This effectively made it illegal to worship in anything but a Catholic Church.

All protestants, but especially the Huguenots, were ordered to convert. If you refused to do so, there were four choices: spend the rest of your life in prison...or on a slave galley, be killed, or escape from the country.

Jean le Cesna was a young Huguenot who had served the French Cavalry, in the Huguenot Regiment commanded by Duke Fredreck de Schomberg. When Schomberg (a Huguenot) quit France, Cesna did also.

Schomberg formed a brigade of Huguenot Calvary for Prince William of Orange. In service for William, these men fought at the Battle of River Boyne, Ireland in 1690. Schomberg was killed. And his Huguenot regiment was disbanded.

Left with no choice but to accept a lease for land in Ulster Ireland, Jean Cesna started life over. He married and raised a family.

In 1718, two of his sons joined the migration of Scotts, Irish and Huguenots from Ireland to America.

Stephen and John Cessna, landed in New Castle, Pennsylvania. Their story is one of starting over in a strange land.

CHAPTER ONE
Starting over

Dublin, Ireland
August 1st, 1690

"It's the Dissenter's Parade!" He spit; then laughed. He pronounced the middle syllable as "SIN."

The shout came from among small group of men standing outside a pub on the road to Drogheda.

"**Dissenters!**" And he said it with all the venom of the worst curse he could imagine. *Dissenters* was a slur given by Catholics to all who rejected faith in the Roman Church. The group of men making a pilgrimage down the road in front of the pub, were Dissenters.

Jean Cesna looked around him.

He and his fellow travelers looked every bit the part of a defeated army. Ninety plus men, of varying ages and languages, hung their heads and drug their feet in a slow amble towards a place their hearts did not seek.

A month ago, they had been victorious soldiers of a Holy War. They shouted and thumped each other on the back in congratulations. It had been the greatest day of their lives. They felt invincible.

Today they had been cast aside by the very King they had served. They were the "unwanted."

On July 12^{th,} the Battle of Boyne River had been an immense success for the protestant armies of William of Orange. He defeated the Catholic forces of King James. It meant that Great Britain would remain free of control by the Pope.

However, that freedom was not to be shared equally.

If the Anglican leaders hated the Papists; they hated other Protestants only a bit less. The Church of England had no intention of letting the other reformers have a part in their power. The Huguenots and Presbyters who helped defeat the Catholics, were now being disarmed and set out of the military.

Anxious to reduce his payroll, these men were the first King William pensioned/discharged from the Army. They were being abandoned before they had even left the field of battle.

Jean Cesna had been told that as a Huguenot he was not allowed free passage back to England. Nor was he allowed free passage back to Belgium where he had first joined the Army.

Instead he was offered a small cash pension, and a chance to settle in Ulster (the protestant counties of Northern Ireland).

The Scotch-Irish Presbyters were offered the same opportunity. As intended, their cash pension was not large enough to purchase passage away from Ireland. They were stranded and abandoned.

Throughout August and September of 1690, 12,000 men were discharged, disarmed, and sent packing. One thousand of those were French Noblemen of the Huguenot Faith.

They wandered to the North in groups of one hundred or less. This group included Jean Cesna, other Huguenots, some Scotts, and a number of the Irish Presbyterians.

They would face derisive calls from bystanders all along the 160-mile walk from Dublin to Belfast. It was a long and miserable walk. The entire way they were greeted with derision by Catholic Irishmen who deeply resented their victory over beloved King James.

The Protestant veterans had been promised to receive a glorious welcome at the end of their journey. But in Belfast, they were considered 2nd class citizens.

The majority of these men had been infantry. Having to surrender their weapons as "property of the King," they carried few possessions. These men had only the clothes on their back.

Cesna was more fortunate. As a member of the light Cavalry under the Duke de Schomberg, he had a horse and a tattered tent. The few utensils for comfort which he carried in his pack were near the end of their life cycle. They were his individual property and did not belong to the King.

Jean had once been a wealthy Noble. But five years of war had consumed every bit of the money he had brought from his home. He had once had a servant to manage his equipment and camp. Now he was on his own, with very few possessions and almost no money.

Cesna had been a part of the Huguenot Cavalry Brigade that Schomberg lead in the French Army. Jean had fought with Schomberg for two years in the southern mountains of Catalonia. In those days, they had been the pride of the French Army.

When Louis IVX repealed the Edict of Nantes in 1685, Schomberg and a large number of his Huguenot troops left the country. Within months, they joined the army of William of Orange to fight against the France's Catholic Army.

Jean Cesna had started his military service as a hero of his homeland, only to become labeled as a traitor to his King.

Now, Cesna felt impoverished and ashamed. He had no country. His beloved Duke was dead, so he had no great cause to serve. He would never again see the green rolling hills of his home in Normandie. He would never see his family again.

Jean Cesna was now a man without an Army to serve. He was a man without a home. He was a man who had no clear future.

Once he had a beautiful cavalry steed. Now he had a worn out beast loaded with his last remaining possessions. He walked slowly, leading the beast, and thinking of the luxury he had known as a boy.

His parents had been Lords of a modest estate in Normandie. They served at the pleasure of the French King. As the official stewards of the land, they enjoyed the best that it had to offer.

Jean remembered his bed, and longed for it. He had slept on nothing but the ground and pallets since leaving Chateau le Cesne six years prior.

Sometimes, he dreamed he was still in combat. The light cavalrymen were the "tip of the spear" for the army. Frequently, they would swoop into a battle and "save the day." Even more frequently, they were treated like heroes at country taverns and military campfires.

Jean always woke from those dreams to the stark reality that his days of good living were over. He had been a cavalry man since his 18th year. For six years he had been in the service of Schomberg.

Now, just 24 years old, he had no future to dream about.

Schomberg was more than a military genius. He was a vocal promoter of Religious Tolerance and had championed the rights of Huguenots in the courts of Europe. Cesna was certain that the old General would never have allowed such treatment of his troops, were he still alive.

But Schomberg was dead. Jean had watched him die.

The General had been caught alone in the middle of the River Boyne. His horse floundering, and his men unable to reach his side, he was cut down by a handful of the enemy.

In a fit of rage, the Huguenot Cavalry had charged into the fray at Old Bridge, turning back the soldiers of King James.

Jean Cesna and his comrades had been heralded as Heroes of the Battle on that day. Their charge had turned the tide of the campaign for Prince William.

Now, William considered them as liabilities.

His champion gone, Cesna began to lose heart.

Two weeks after the death of Duke Schomberg, it was announced that King William had no intention of invading France. This had been promised to them when they first joined William's army. But the Huguenots in Schomberg's cavalry were not going home to free their families.

Cesna was fortunate in that his weapons, equipment, and horse were his private property and had not been issued by the army. He at least had these to start over. But the old man who was his servant had abandoned him shortly after King William did.

Like the others in this column of desolate men, Jean Cesna was defeated. But he was not yet broken. With almost nothing, having lost more than men should bear, this group of veterans started down an unknown road to an unpromising future.

Though not having actually fought at each other's side; these men would become Brothers-in-Arms on that long walk North. Jean's skills at English were rudimentary. Still, he was embraced by these men who spoke that language with heavy Scottish and Irish accents.

They supported each other on their journey. At their campfires each evening of the march, they began to formulate dreams of a new beginning for each of them. These were men who would contribute to each other's fortune for the rest of their days.

Their old lives were forever lost. Somehow, these old soldiers were all being reborn on this long walk to a future they could barely imagine.

Bone-weary from battle, many of the men had failing shoes and coats. It would take 16 days for the group to make the 160-mile walk to Belfast.

The group was slowed because they refused to leave the weaker ones behind, keeping pace to accommodate the wounded and elderly among them.

Unwilling expatriates of France, soldiers without an army that needed them, deprived of the support of family and their church leaders.... A lot of the Huguenot refugees began to fall apart.

A number had taken to drink in their despair. Others began to steal from the populace when they were hungry or cold. Many of these men soon languished in the prisons of Dublin and Belfast. They would receive no sympathy from English Justice.

As Jean Cesne looked back on the past year. It seemed that this terrible end had been cursed to pass from the start.

Initially, they joined Prince William in Belgium. They fought the Catholic Armies of France and Spain for several years. The fighting was at a standstill when a new offer came to Prince William.

In England, the Protestant nobles outnumbered the Catholic ones. Forcing King James from the throne, they invited Prince William to come and assume the Crown.

William's invasion of England was met with little opposition. He immediately discharged all of the non-Englishmen of his Army because he could not pay them. They were abandoned in the countryside around London. English nobles complained to William that they were making problems for the local people.

But King James was not ready to quit.

James was given a new army by the King of France and landed in Ireland. His plan was to gradually reconquer all of the British Isles.

William called his recently discharged army back into service. Duke Schomberg reorganized his Huguenot Cavalry. Jean Cesna joined for a second time.

From England, they organized, and made "a glorious invasion" of Ireland at Carrick Fergus. However, Jean had been sickened by the "ingloriousness of it all."

There was little honor in their conduct. The English army was more of an infestation than an invasion. Disorganization was rampant. This was not the civilized army which the French were proud of.

Schomberg's Cavalry had left their horses in England. Someone had failed to arrange transport for the creatures. As soon as they landed, each cavalryman dashed into the countryside to procure mounts in any way possible: purchase, barter, theft, murder, and confiscation.

Jean would never tell his sons how he had gotten his own mount, but the poor beast would have been more at home behind a plow than as a war steed.

The Huguenot battalion was made up mostly of young nobles, all of whom wanted to be officers. So each of the five companies had two captains, two lieutenants, two ensigns, and so on. Command was a quagmire of confusion.

Schomberg made an extremely poor choice for their place of encampment. He thought it wise to put a swamp at their back, hoping to provide defense against a surprise attack.

This left only half of their perimeter needing defense and eased the manpower needs. He thought this wise because the majority of his battalion were wealthy noblemen who did not want to serve guard duty, and were frequently absent when they were to be on watch.

Instead of providing safety, the mosquitoes of that swamp claimed the lives of one third of his troops. The camp was a chaotic mess of starvation and sickness. Schomberg had failed to organize any sanitation.

Jean's faith nearly failed him several times in those weeks of waiting.

Then the battle came on July 12, 1690. It would be named after the river that separated the two armies.

Confusion was rampant. Someone said that the river before them was the Boyne. The only way Jean could tell friend from enemy was by what side of that river they were on.

No one could tell them where they were supposed to be. And each officer and soldier had his own opinion about what they should do.

Jean's cavalry unit just rode back and forth along the river, looking for a good place to attack. It was a game of "chicken." Whoever entered the water first would become an easy target from the opposing army.

They watched in horror as Marshall Schomberg fell from his horse into the river. He had charged into the current ahead of his troops. The old commander was quickly surrounded by Ennishkillers. In minutes they took his life.

The cavalry men became crazed with anger at the death of their hero, and charged ahead... in all directions at once.

That day Jean had no clear purpose, other than kill every Papist he could find. No one was more surprised to find Cesna still alive at the end of the day, than Jean himself.

The stink of blood and death would stay in his nose for weeks. His clothing was never completely clean again.

Jean was stunned that men were capable of such gore and brutality. This was not the dignified fighting he had been trained for. This was hack and chop, anyone who came in front of you, even if their back was turned.

How can God be pleased with this? Jean asked himself.

Now, sitting at his miserable campfire, Jean Cesna was even more convinced that God had not been pleased with his actions. It seemed certain that he was being punished.

Now the war was over. Now they were among the rejected. The march from Dundalk was humiliating and embarrassing.

CHAPTER TWO

Belfast Harbor, 18 September 1690

Land Agents had arranged themselves near the docks in the Ulster capital. They had no love for this land, and sought to return to England as quickly as their task was accomplished.

London investors formed groups and purchased large tracts of Ulster land from King William. This was how the Prince of Orange had managed to pay for his war.

By selling land confiscated from Catholic lords and business owners to investors, the King raised the cash he needed. And now he found a place to plant the no-longer-needed soldiers. They would be far away from London.

There had been fears that the large Army in Ireland might just turn on William and re-invade England in their anger at being cast aside.

Jean Cesna waited in line to present his discharge certificate to the Land Agent. He was asked if he preferred to live in the city or the country. He chose the country. He knew country life better.

In France, Jean's family managed a large estate which produced fine wines, magnificent horses, and an abundance of grain.

Many of the Huguenots and Scotsman would choose city lots or houses once owned by Catholics. Others, chose to live close to the land and renew their souls with physical labor.

Cesna was handed a lease. It was to a farm of five acres about 20 miles from the city. The lease was at a very modest £4 yearly rent, and guaranteed at that price for 25 years.

Having no choice, the former cavalryman signed a 25-year agreement to work the land offered him.

Jean Cesna found his farm to be long neglected and abandoned. It had been home to a Catholic family. It was obvious that this family had been keenly set in the mentality that poverty is a virtue. It had no comforts of any kind other than a semblance of a roof.

The family had done little to improve the place. Portions of the walls were incomplete. The house was one room, and smelled horrible.

Jean Cessna sat on the stone hearth and looked around at the pitiful excuse of a house.

He was home. He was alone.

He was more penniless than he had ever been in his life. He was indeed at the lowest point he had ever known any person to be.

Hungry, cold, without even a pallet to lie on, Jean fell to the ground. Tears of quiet despair burdened his eyes into sleep.

A bright sun greeted him the next day. His weary body climbed to his feet and surveyed the situation around him. He was starting from the poorest place he had ever been.

CHAPTER THREE
County Lurgan, Ireland

Jean had named the horse "Claudine." Her breed was hard to determine, but she seemed an obvious fit for the plow. She certainly had been of very dubious service as a cavalry mount.

Jean Cesna had joined Schomberg's cavalry with a horse he had raised from a colt. It was a fine cavalry mount and had been trained by him. Together they made a formidable combat team.

All of the men in Schomberg's Brigade were noblemen. Jean Cesna was the second son of a Baron. His older brother would inherit the land. Jean's best future lay with a military career or the priesthood. He chose the first.

The cavalry had to provide their own horses and equipment. It required a good deal of wealth to be a member of that elite fighting force.

Jean would never be reunited with the valuable beast that had been his partner for half his life. "Sabre" was lost to the fortunes of war, along with most everything else he had invested in what he believed was a noble cause. The nobility of that cause had slowly faded with every month he served.

Landing in Dundalk, the cavalry men had spread out across the countryside, "acquiring" mounts in any form or fashion they could manage. "Claudine" had been found grazing in a field, and Jean was once again a mounted warrior.

She was a total opposite of his "Sabre." She was slow, plodding, and gentle. Her gait was such that it would break a man's back if he stayed in the saddle too long. He guessed her age at near fifteen, and prayed she would carry him to the battle even if she could not participate in the fighting.

Claudine was now his only companion. Together they stood looking out over the stony fields of his new home.

It was going to take so much work, and so there was little time. It was already late Summer and no crop had been planted. It was going to be a hungry Winter. It was overwhelming just to contemplate what needed to be done.

Gentle and accommodating Claudine showed no reluctance to the task. Somehow, this gave Jean the courage to make a start.

In the garden, he found "volunteer" cabbage and herbs for tea. Nothing had been deliberately cultivated for over a year.

In the field, he found sparsely scattered stalks of oats that had somehow sprung from seeds dropped in the last harvest. With meticulous gleaning, he salvaged a meager amount to feed himself.

Claudine had a bigger appetite. The grass was enough for now, but he needed to store fodder for the winter or she would perish.

And there was an additional problem.

He suspected the old girl might be with foal.

Normally, cavalry mounts were gelded and could be corralled with fillies without worrying about this. But a few of the new the horses pressed into service had shown an interest in breeding every female in the corral. Jean was certain that his new partner had received such attention.

Soon, there might be two horses to feed through the hungry months. And all of them needed a better shelter.

Jean collected stone from the field, and clay from the nearby creek. Building three walls and a roof he added a room to the cottage. Eventually it would be a bedroom, but for now it would serve as a stable.

In his pack of camping equipment, Jean had just one cup and two plates made of tin. A single iron pot was used to heat water for bathing, and then for making stew.

Using the same clay he used for the walls, Jean fashioned pots to hold things. These he dried on the hearth. Not having a kiln; they were not going to last many months before they needed replacement.

Jean Cesna needed tools. He needed flour for the winter. But he had little money. His pitifully small pension had been mostly spent feeding himself on the journey from the South.

A two-day trip back to Belfast enabled him to trade his saddle and spurs for a plow and harness.

The sword, which had been his grandfather's, was traded for a scythe and other tools. He was now a farmer and no longer a warrior.

He purchased only one luxury while on his shopping mission, a small apple. It was his first taste of sweet in months.

With great care, he salvaged every seed from the fruit. Planting them in small pots. indoors, he managed to get three seedlings which would be the start of an orchard. These required very tender care, and would not bear fruit for five years. Jean was beginning to plan in terms of years instead of weeks.

With no one to help except Claudine, Jean cleared stone from the field and planted his first few rows of Oats. A small garden plot was set with more cabbage. The stones he pried from the soil were added to the perimeter walls and the room he was building.

With the scythe, he harvested as much hay as he could for the winter ahead. It provided bedding for both he and his partner, and would feed the latter in the lean months.

The scythe also enabled him to harvest rushes from the river. Jean used those to rethatch his roof. Then he made a roof for the new room. Everything he needed had to be built from scratch, using only the hammer and saw he had traded his sword for. Crude furniture soon graced his tiny home.

Jean Cessna had not been able to part with the fourteen inch dagger his father had given him. It was now pressed into service for both kitchen and carpentry tasks.

The work was overwhelming. The solitude was oppressive, but it was also healing for his grieving soul. He had lost so much. And the work gave him a feeling that he was slowly regaining what he had lost. The progress seemed slow in coming. But each accomplishment encouraged him a little.

During that first winter there was no money for a weekly trip to the pub. The teas he made himself were created from local herbs and wild plants. They flavored and purified drinking water, but offered no luxury.

Hunger was a constant companion. The cold winds of Northern Ireland continually tempted him to abandon all hope.

The days were short, and the lonely nights were long. The cold was often unbearable. The only source of fuel for the fire was peat. He had to dig this from the bog and dry it in his yard.

Somehow, Jean survived.

Spring found a much-improved farm, though there was still much to do. The stone wall had been completed around one entire paddock.

Jean could now plant a much larger plot for oats. This year he would plant turnips which he might market. His kitchen garden would be much bigger this year also.

He and Claudine spent three days plowing the field for a neighbor. In exchange, he received four ducklings (hopefully one would be male) and a female piglet. Next winter he would not have to rely on just catching wild rabbit and fish to put meat in his stew.

By June, Jean Cesna had improved the farm enough that he was able to enjoy the sabbath day of rest once again. Claudine needed it as much as he.

Jean had survived his first year. The farm was now improved enough to feed him and the livestock. But it still had not yielded any kind of cash.

The £4 annual rent was due in September. He had to find a way to make cash or his labor would be lost for lack of the rent.

In his most discouraged moment, Jean looked into the small fire and asked, *Is this my reward for serving God?*

He was progressively losing the strength of his moral fiber to the numerous storms of his life.

Looking back at his life he took stock of the road he had traveled. For six years he fully expected to die in battle on any day. He fought without any reserve or regard for his own life.

He lived to serve God, engaged in the struggle of religious freedom. In his time, military service and the priesthood were equal commitments to God. Politics and religion were so interwoven that they could not be told apart.

Jean had never dreamed of building a personal life and family. That would be too selfish when God needed warriors.

He was prepared to lay his life on the altar of Truth, as God has appointed him to do. God had destined him to be a sacrifice in this Holy War.

Some things he had been absolutely sure of. Now, sitting alone in a frigid stone hut, he was no longer sure about anything.

CHAPTER FOUR
Culbertson's Pub

The most reliable thing about a thatch roof is that it needs constant repair.

In the city, there were no fields or streams to gather the materials. Cesna learned he could generate tiny amounts of coin by harvesting the materials needed for the roofs in the city. He used Claudine to haul them into town.

Every spare hour of July and August was spent in the hot sun cutting reeds and rush for thatch. These were tied tightly into roofing bundles, and stacked high. On week Market Day, he and Claudine carried large loads to the city. A few shillings at a time, he raised the rent money.

When the turnip crop came in, he hauled that to market as well. Now, he had a tiny treasury to build his security on. The cottage began to fill with small luxuries like a lantern for candles, a wash bowl and pitcher, socks to cushion his feet from the leather boots; and his first new set of underlinens in four years.

After a year with no money, Jean felt so wealthy that he added a new routine to his weekly activities. On Saturday night, he took himself to the pub.

There he enjoyed a bowl of hearty Irish Stew and a single pint of ale. It cost a couple of pence and was the only extravagance he allowed himself.

This weekly ritual allowed Jean Cesna to reenter the human race. After a year of isolation, he renewed acquaintances with his friends from the "Dissenter's Parade."

Several of them had settled on farms around him. The overwhelming amount of labor required to survive the first winter had not allowed for any social time.

His weekly trips to the pub provided another opportunity which he could not have foreseen.

Mary Kathleen (her real name is unknown) was the daughter of the village cordwainer. On Saturday's, she worked as a server in the pub to manage the larger crowd. More of the bachelor farmers were coming for a weekly meal.

Mary Kate was "taken" by this handsome man with the pale blue eyes. His French accent helped to set him apart from the other patrons. He had the manners of a Nobleman. Most of her customers were rough Scots and Irishmen.

At six-foot, Jean was one of the few men who had to bow when coming through the front door. His Saxon features made him a rarity in the Scotch-Irish crowd. Even among his fellow Frenchmen his features had been a rarity.

Mary Kate loved to tease him about his "big" ears. Indeed, his ears seem to be about 20% larger than average. And the upper part tended to lean away from the head making them more obvious. Not ugly or distracting; it was noticeable and distinct.

And in the middle of his forehead, one tuft of hair tended to fall in a curl. Jean had a nervous habit of trying to brush it back into place, only to have it soon fall back across his brow.

Mostly, the Irish lass had been touched by the loneliness which hovered over this handsome man. It may have struck a maternal instinct in her heart. She determined to herself that she would make this man laugh at his every visit to the pub.

Jean received a greater share of her flirtation, than did the other patrons. This was not missed by the other men, even if Jean was slow to recognize it.

By September of 1692, Jean Cesna had improved his farm to the point it was supporting himself and yielding a cash profit. And Mary Kate had convinced him that he needed her attention on a more frequent basis.

At the end of his second year, Jean felt secure enough that he could ask her to marry.

On their wedding day, she moved a considerable amount of cooking and household items into the cottage. She also brought a bed, the first he had touched since leaving home.

She brought two other things as well.

Mary Cathleen brought her Irish Spinning Wheel into the Cesna home. And she brought a 1/2 lb. bag of flax seed.

"From now on we will grow Flax in the East field." She announced. "And I will sell the threads I make to the weavers in Belfast."

With that, the Cesna family became a tiny part of the growing textile manufacturing industry of Northern Ireland.

Mary Kate had been producing materials for her father's cord making business. Now she intended to provide threads for fine linens and lace.

The Cesna household was well on its way to a thriving lifestyle as both Mary Kate and John (as she now called him) began to work in a partnership. They focused their labors on a single vision.

It was about this time that John began to spell his last name with a double "S" to indicate the hard sound his family preferred. It made it easier for the English and Irish to pronounce his name.

Laughter returned to his life. And hope.

CHAPTER FIVE
Cessna Farm
December 1693

The arrival of Mary Kate in his home seemed to transform everything in John Cessna's life. The home was filled with music and laughter. Somehow the cottage always seemed warmer than it had before; and somehow it also always felt cooler in the summer.

The farm began to prosper as well. The pastures fairly exploded with grass to feed the beasts and provide hay for the winter. One field yielded an abundance of oats, with turnips planted in the same field following the grain harvest. Another field provided an amazing crop of flax.

John had thought that field too wet and marshy for a decent crop. But flax seemed to thrive in those conditions.

From the flax could come a coarse thread used to sew canvas for ship sails. From the finer fibers came thread that was used to make linens and lace. It was by far the crop which yielded the most cash profit.

The ducks had grown into a large flock and provided meat on a regular basis. The piglet had grown into a healthy sow. That summer she provided her second litter. The first had been only six, the second was a dozen new piglets.

John's meager garden had become a cornucopia of vegetables, spices, and teas under the magical touch of Mary Kate.

The Frenchman, now in his 27th year, could hardly believe the prosperity that had come to him.

The greatest and most miraculous blessing came in the first week of December in 1793. John and Mary Kate celebrated the arrival of a son, Stephen Cessna. The child was named after her father.

Mary Kate was overjoyed with delivering her first child. John was in awe.

He could find no words in either English or French to describe the happiness he was experiencing.

Sitting in the family hearth, carefully studying every feature of the tiny human creature before him...John was overwhelmed with unfamiliar feelings. He was a father!

"You know, Mr. Cessna," said Mary Kate. "The day you decided to become a soldier, and a destroyer of things, this world began to strip possessions away from you.

"But the day you decided to sell your sword and work the soil, Our Lord began to add things back to your life. Every week has added to your wealth and happiness."

John pondered the words carefully. He knew she was right on many levels.

"Your dynasty, is not in a chateau or estate of land in France. It is not in a title or inheritance." His wife continued. She had heard him lament about his boyhood home on far too many evenings.

"Your dynasty is in that child who holds your finger. I can see a long line of blue eyed, fair haired children, with ears just a bit too big, coming forth from the love in this humble home."

Jean was not able to see that same vision.

William was born in the fall of 1695. He came with green eyes like his mother, and a faint reddish tint to his hair. John, Jr. joined the family in 1698. And John Cessna Jr. would be their last child. Two other children had not survived their births.

Infant John looked like a duplicate of his father. He even had the adorable curl of hair which fell down across his forehead.

As the three boys filled the cottage, energetically vying for their mother's attention, Jean Cessna began to see what Mary Kate had seen.

The house was still filled with music and singing. But it was also filled with tiny demanding voices.

Shortly after Stephen was born, Claudine lay down for her last time. Her filly now took her place as the strongest member of the Cessna family.

Jean named her Marie. He told Mary Kate it was the name of his mother. But in reality, it was the name of a young dark-haired French girl he had fancied in his youth.

CHAPTER SIX
Christmas Eve 1717

John threw all his weight behind the blow he leveled at his brother's chin. The impact succeeded in throwing them both to the floor.

Leaping to his feet in triumph, John glared down at Stephen. Although fisticuffs and insults were a part of the daily affection they bestowed on each other, this was the first time that John had gotten the best of his older and larger brother.

On the verge of manhood at 17 years, John Cessna, Jr. could not have felt any more powerful.

Then, the lights went out.

He awoke to see his brother, Stephen, cowering with his back to the fireplace, his hands defending his face.

Their father stood before him holding a dented pot, bellowing in anger.

"C'est Noel. Tis Christmas! No fighting. Mon Dieu!" he roared. "Peace and love only on this day," and he threw the pot which had offended John's head, to the far side of the room.

With exasperation, John Cessna Sr. sank back into his chair and returned to the bitter mood which had enveloped him for weeks now. He was growing old. He was growing tired.

John Cessna was now sixty. The harsh Irish life made him look 20 years older than that.

"Bitter mood" was the old Frenchman's usual demeanor these days. This land grew more uncooperative as the years passed. Life continued to cheat him a bit more as he watched the Christmases drag by.

"It is mine!" hissed Stephen at his brother.

"Says you!" returned his younger brother with just as much venom.

The article in question was a small steel knife that had previously belonged to William, their deceased brother. The issue of its inheritance had become a daily drama for the boys.

"Will promised to sell it to me," proclaimed Stephen. "He never liked you much, and he never would have given it to you."

"Well, you weren't there when that horse kicked him in the head." John had no intention of yielding on this point.

"Yeah, isn't it funny no one else heard him give it to you, but YOU. How did that horse happen to kick him in the head anyway? Weren't you holding the reigns?"

John Jr. looked as though he had been dealt another blow. Fire lit up his eyes and he glared. "You were supposed to be there but you said you was sickly!"

The knife was a simple thing. It was nearly worn out. But it was still a functional tool. It was a perfect size to hide inside your belt, and to provide help when needed. And young men frequently have need of a sharp blade.

The blade had little actual value; but for Stephen, the smaller the value of something being fought over, the more bitter the fight.

Both boys knew the blade's true origin. It was the broken point of a fourteen inch dagger that Jean's father had given him 30 years earlier.

The knife had a strange way of appearing and disappearing. John Jr. would have it for a few days, then it would vanish.

A week later, Stephen would "find" it and be discovered employing it in some small task. A subsequent battle for its possession ensued, resulting in it vanishing again. Then it reappeared in John's hand.

The boys were squaring off for another round of debate when the door opened, and their mother entered from her daily trip to the garden. It looked like they were going to eat cabbage soup again.

Their instant and profound silence told her that something was amiss. Within moments she found the dented pot. Her lips tsking softly, she carried it to her husband and simply said,

"I will need that dent straightened by supper time."

"Par Dieu! C'est Noël." he muttered aloud.

French was father's intimate language. All paternal advice and condemnation came to the boys in that language. Education, both secular and religious, was imposed in the language of home as well. French was more cultured than English!

Their father was the only parent who had received an education. He was their school master, and reasoned that they would learn enough English from the neighbors. But they were still Frenchmen. Real reason was that he still thought in French and it was easier to access his memories through that medium.

Jean's weekly Bible lessons were all from the French Bible given to him by his father four decades earlier.

English and Gaelic, they would learn from their mother. French would be in their hearts.

John Cessna Sr.'s first decade on this land had been somewhat prosperous.

He had no way of knowing that Europe was at the beginning of The Little Ice Age and the years of fruitful agriculture were behind them. Winters were getting longer and harsher. Some years, it was like there was no summer at all.

Agriculture in England and Ireland changed dramatically in the first 15 years of the 18th Century. Where once they had grown grapes and succulents, now they could only grow those grains which could withstand the harsh cold.

Life was filled with bone crushing toil and frequent illnesses. His family was being decimated by hunger and disease. Mary Kate had lost two children. John was certain it was because of their poor diet and hard lives.

Their warmth came by burning the foul-smelling peat they dug from the enormous bogs. When dried in the yard around the house it could be burned instead of wood. It was a long way to the nearest forest.

John Cessna felt like he was watching the lives of his family drain slowly into this unforgiving soil. Mary Kate was growing frailer each month.

Many of his fellow Huguenot soldiers had settled in the cities and helped start the textile industries. They were prospering much better than those who took country estates.

Mary Kate had moved the Cessna family into the world of textiles with her vision for growing flax and spinning threads both fine and coarse. Stephen and John, Jr. had both acquired spinning wheels and helped in the work during the long winter days.

Stephen and John, Jr. seemed fit for nothing more than farm labor and managing the livestock. But it was rare they could complete a day's labor without a round of conflict.

William had been more easy-going and amiable. He was of his mother's temperament, whereas the other boys resembled their adventurous and head strong father in his youthful days.

Those ways had changed for Jean/John Cessna. A cavalryman in his youth, he had traded that life for a peaceful life of caring for the land. His temper was seldom seen now that he had reached his sixties.

But these were times that could break a man.

The changing weather had diminished the profits of his farm business. And September brought come the harshest news of all.

The 25-year lease the veterans had received, was ending. It was a reasonable £4 per year. And in an average year a farmer of ten acres could expect to make about £20-22 from his labor.

The London investment groups which owned the land felt that the farms had increased in value. This was true largely because of the work ethic of the Scotch-Irish and Huguenot tenants.

John Cessna had been informed that beginning next year, his rent would rise to £15. It was a blow that nearly killed him.

He took his case to the local magistrate, and received his second shock. All his Presbyterian and Huguenot neighbors had been removed from their positions in local government. "The Test Act" had been passed by Parliament that year.

It said simply, that to hold any government office, one had to pass the test of taking communion in the Anglican Church. This became a political statement signifying that you considered the King of England to also be the Head of the Church on Earth.

The new rules even said that they had to use Anglican priests to baptize, marry or bury their children. Their own ministers had no legal standing because of The Test Act.

These veterans had defeated the Catholic Army, only to be pensioned to Ulster by King William. Now they felt even more betrayed than ever. Their complaints were raised as loud as old men can manage.

But they were too old to take up arms and make the situation right. Despair again became the seasoning for every meal in the Cessna cottage.

"Carry me to the pub!" declared John Cessna. The boys knew this meant that they would have to hurry to keep up with him on the way to the pub; but they might actually have to carry him home again.

Mary Kate would have the cottage to herself, and not have to worry much about supper. It suited her since tomorrow was the holiday and she had much to do in preparation.

Through the biting wind, John pushed with a heart that was weary and beaten. The two sons followed, excited for what might lie ahead.

Whiskey might be their only real warmth this evening; whiskey and the companionship of other men who shared their hard life. And maybe, just maybe, thought the boys, they might see a good fight.

CHAPTER SEVEN
Culbertson's Pub

It was a perfect Christmas Eve celebration.

The pub was a smoky cavern of bitter men, roaring like beasts; complaining, promising woe on their enemies, gambling, whispering lurid stories, and celebrating that for all their other lacking, at least they were MEN.

Not a woman or child was in sight. The young men were loud with their braggadocio. The old men used wit to deflate the younger egos.

Every stomach was soon graced with the wild rabbit stew which old man Culbertson had managed to produce.

Only one man had his nose broken for him that evening. It was still a wonderful and righteous commemoration of the Birth of our Blessed Savior.

Culbertson's was a decent Protestant Pub, thank you very much!

It was about midnight when Alexander Culbertson called the crowd to quiet and announced the event which would change everything. He had received a letter from his nephew in America.

"America" commanded a powerful fascination for them all. It held them in rapt attention.

Although it was addressed to the family, in a sense, it was addressed to all who lived in their village. Such letters became public estate.

With all the pomp and reverence of a Sunday sermon, Alex Culbertson was going to recite it to the fine gentlemen of this district. Every weathered face in the place was turned in eager anticipation. Here, after all, was an epistle from another world.

(Editor's note: This letter was written by John

Valentine to his sister and family in 1725. It is presented in his own style of writing with some corrections.)

Dear Sister Mary Valentine,
    "The letter was addressed to my niece, but you will want to hear it all the same," announced Culbertson. And he continued.

This goes with a Salutation of Love to thee, Brother Thomas & the children, & in a word, to all our friends, Relations, and Well Wishers in general as if I had named them. I hope it may find you all in good health, as I with all our family in general are in at this present writing & and has been since our arrival. For we have not had a day's sickness in the family since we came to this county, blessed be God for it. My father in particular has not had his health better these ten years than since he came here, even with his ancient age considered. Our Irish acquaintance in general are well, except Thos. Lightfoot, who departed this life in Darby in a good age about 4 weeks since.

Culbertson paused here to announce, "Old Sean Valentine is the saintliest man you ever met. God bless him for his good health!" And he paused to wipe a tear from his eye before he read further.

Thee writes in thy letter that there was talk went back to Ireland that we were not satisfied in coming here, which is utterly false. Now let this suffice to convince you. In the first place he that carried back this story was an idle fellow, & one of our shipmates. Not thinking this country suitable to his idleness; went back with Cowman again. He is sort of a lawyer, or rather a liar as I term him, Therefore I would not have you give credit to such false reports for the future, for there is not one of the family but what likes the country very well. And if we were in Ireland would again come here directly. It is the best country for working folk and tradesmen of any in the world. But for Drunkards and Idlers, they cannot live well anywhere. It is likewise an extraordinarily healthy country.

Land is of all prices, even from 10 pounds to one hundred pounds a hundred acre, according to the goodness or else the situation thereof. It grows dearer every year by reason of vast quantities of people that come here yearly from several parts of the world. Therefore thee & thy family or any that I wish well I would desire to make what speed you can to come here the sooner the better.

We have traveled over a pretty deal of this country to seek for land and we met with many fine tracts of land here & there in the country. Yet my father being curious & somewhat hard to please did not buy any land until the second day of 10th month. And then he bought a tract of land consisting of five hundred acres, for which he gave 350 pounds. It is excellent good land but none cleared, except about 20 acres, with a small log house & orchard planted. We are going to clear some of it directly, for our next summer's fallow. We might have bought land much cheaper but not so much to our satisfaction. We stayed in Chester 3 months & then rented a place 1 mile from Chester, with a good brick house & 200 acres of land for (3) pounds a year where we continue till next May.

We have sowed about 200 acres of wheat & 7 acres of rye. This season we sowed but a bushel an acre, 3 pecks is enough on new ground. I am grown an experienced plow and & my brother Abell is learning. Jonathan & thy son John drives for us he is grown a lusty fellow since thou saw him, we have the finest plows that can be. We plowed up our summer fallows in May & June, with a yoak of Oxen & 2 horses. And they go with as much ease as double the number in Ireland. We sow our wheat with 2 horses. A boy of 12 or 14 years old can hold the plow here. A man commonly holds and drives himself, they plow an acre, nay some plows 2 acres a day, they sow wheat and Rye in August or September.

Alex paused until the crowd stopped murmuring in amazement at the sobering vision created by these words. The stony soil of Ireland allowed a man to plow but ½ acre in a day.

We have had crops of oats, barley & very good flax & hemp. Indian Corn & buckwheat all of our own sowing and planting this last summer. We also planted a bushel of white potatoes which cost us 5 shills, & we had 10 or 12 bushels increase, this country yields extraordinary increase of all sorts of grain.

Likewise for Nicholas Hooper had 3 acres of land & at almost 3 bushels of seed above 80 bushels increase so that it is as plentiful a country as can be if people will be industrious.

"80 to 3 increase!" shouted old man Naugle. "It's a damn lie! I ain't ever got more than 4 to 1." And the crowd joined together in hushing him.

Wheat is 4 shills a bushel, rye is 2 sh. 9 d, Oats, 2.3 pence, barley 3 shills, Indian corn 2 Shills all strike measure. Beef is 2 1/2 pence a pound sometimes more sometimes less. Mutton 2 1/2, pork 2 1/2 per pound. Turnips 12 pence a bushel heaps' measure & so plenty that an acre produces 200 bushels.

All sorts of provisions are extraordinary plenty in Philadelphia market, where country people bring in their commodities. Their markets are on the 4th and 7th weekdays. This country abounds in fruit, scarce a house but has an Apple, Peach & Cherry orchard. As for chestnuts, Walnuts & hazel nuts, Strawberries, Bilberries & Mulberries; they grow wild in the woods & fields in vast quantities. They also make great preparations against harvest; both roast & boiled.

Cakes & tarts & rum, stand at the land's end, so workers may eat and drink at pleasure. A reaper has 2 shills & 3 pence a day, a mower has 2 shills and 6 pence and a pint of rum besides meat and drink of the best. For no workman works without their victuals in the bargain throughout the country. A laboring man has 18 or 20 pence a day in winter.

"Heavenly God! A man could get rich," murmured someone in the back of the room. And the entire room began to mutter in their wonder.

It was now near one in the morning. The crowd murmured as each man absorbed the meaning of what he had just heard. Men had been holding their breath so as to not miss a single word.

It was indeed a different world their neighbors had gone to. It was so far away. It was so mystifying. Yet the letter made it seem so nearby.

Alex Culbertson announced that it was now Christmas Day. He would serve no more Whiskey!

Black ale and stale bread would have to suffice the men on the Holy Day.

It was still six hours before the sun arose. The fine Christian gentlemen of Lurgan would process all that they had learned in the reading of the letter, and ferociously debate if it could really be true. Sometimes they demanded a re-reading of the figures on yields and prices.

The rest of the night they paraphrased what they had heard, enlarging the truth with alcohol.

When the sun was peaking up, the Cessna men made their way home.

They stopped briefly beside the plot which held the body of his son, William and the two wee ones. John

Cessna paused for a long time.

Acidic tears welled in his eyes. Wiping away the moisture, he made a promise to himself.

"I'll not bury another of my children in this bitter land."

His two sons heard his words and looked at each other, thinking it was black beer which was making their father delusional.

CHAPTER EIGHT
Christmas Day

Waking at noon, John found Mary Kate sitting before the fire in her rocking chair. She had tea and a bit of bread waiting for him, and his chair had been pulled close to hers.

The old man feared he was about to be reprimanded for the previous night's drinking. He would soon receive a surprise.

His wife remained silent and stoic until he had finished his third sip of tea. *This will be a bad one*, he thought to himself.

"Our boys have no future in this place," Mary Kate said with a heavy tone in her voice. "They have no way to make a living for themselves. They will never be able to leave our home."

This was not the topic John had expected. It took several moments for him to catch up with her thinking. His wife had obviously been kneading her worries on this topic for a long time.

"They will never be able to afford a wife. We will never have grandchildren if we stay in this place."

Cessna had been focused on the economic and political problems they faced. Mary Kate was looking at the future from other directions; but those seemed just as bleak.

John Cessna wondered if his wife was about to suggest they leave the farm and move to the city. He hated the thought of that.

The rent increase meant that it would be more than difficult to make a yearly profit. The "Test" meant that his every dealing with a government official would be prejudiced against him.

A new rule said that Anglican Priests controlled every aspect of religious life. This was deeply insulting to the veterans. But John was only thinking in the term of a few years.

Now, Mary Kate presented him with the long-term consequences. The fate of their children was being smothered. Without land to work, and a decent profit to be made, none of the boys would ever be able to take a wife. She would never be a grandmother.

After listening to her fears for a good while, Jean

began to tell her about the letter he had heard in the pub the previous evening. Across the county, other men were sharing the same story with their wives on this Christmas Day.

Wives now heard the seductive visions of what life in the Americas could mean for their families. It was like the promise of a cool rain following a long hot spell in Summer.

Christmas Day was celebrated quietly in their home that year. The boys would sleep until late afternoon. And at the evening meal the conversation would be somber.

Leaving the boys to do their chores on the day after Christmas, John headed for the pub. There would be another gathering of old men at the pub.

John's thoughts had been fermenting since the reading of what was now called "The Letter." John had a few questions to ask of his friend, Alexander Culbertson.

Three other men were already gathered in the pub when he pushed through the door. Will Campbell turned to greet him as he entered. But James Dunlap and Michael O'Neal kept their heads bowed listening closely to what the pub keeper was saying.

Without any ceremony, John joined the group and was handed a mug of dark beer.

"The breakfast of old soldiers," he muttered in a prayerful tone as he took his first sip.

These men had been drawn by the same mysterious force. No one had issued an invitation, but each had been pulled to this meeting as if given a personal summons.

Each had the same thing on his mind ... The Letter. Each was driven by the frustration of this ungenerous land.

Each of these men had been planted here by the English settlement of the area. None of them had any roots in this land, save the graves of loved ones who had been sacrificed to it.

"Do you reckon it can be as fair as the lad writes?"

"I wonder if there is still enough land for newcomers."

"I heard the Savage Tribals will sneak into your home at night and cut the throats of your babies."

This last remark brought a hearty laugh from everyone at the table. The laughter faded to silence as the men stared in deep contemplation at the drinks before them.

"I think I have to try for it," announced John Cessna to no one in particular. "It feels like I am supposed to try for it."

His old sense of personal destiny and God's providence had reawakened in him.

"Go on with yourself! You must be a mad man to want to make such a trip at your age." Will Campbell offered. "You've a wife and sons to think of."

"This can't be the place God wants me to build my family," John Cessna added in a quiet tone.

Four faces turned to him in silent surprise. No words were spoken until three full minutes and at least a third of their beverage had disappeared.

It was one of those pivotal moments in a man's life, when he takes a harsh inventory of himself and his possessions. As harsh as it is to be found wanting by another, it is much worse to be found wanting by your own conscience.

This is when a man gets very honest with himself. No time to comfort your pride with your own compliments. John felt he might have one last chance to get things right. There might be one last opportunity to make his life count for something.

"And I," stated Alex Culbertson.

"And I," each of the others slowly added with a reluctant but firm tone, both sure and unsure at the same time. The mood in the room was heavy.

None of them missed the significance of the pledge they had just made to each other ... a promise they were making to themselves.

Not one of them was underestimating the effort and sacrifice it would take. All of these men had been "transplanted" before, so the fear of starting over would not deter them.

All of them knew the dangers, the hardships that came with their decision to follow the lure of a better life.

"Where do we start?" Campbell asked.

"Captain Cowman is spending the winter in

Belfast with his wife. I reckon that when the weather breaks in March or April, he will start another trip to Pennsylvania."

Alexander Culbertson had obviously been giving this some thought. But then, he had held the letter in his hand longer than the others. "One or two of us should go see him and find out what all is needed."

Alex and James Dunlap volunteered for the mission. The others began to make a thorough list of questions for them to ask. What is the cost? What should we bring? How much can we bring? On and on the questions went. There was so much to learn and so much to do.

Their second meeting came a week later when the two scouts returned from their meeting with the ship captain. It took a good six hours and four pints to completely debrief the men. In the end, it was a solo process. Each man had to make his own decision.

The overwhelming obstacle for all of them was the cost. Captain Cowman said the going price was £15 a person. This was nearly ¾ of a man's yearly income. Who could afford such a price?

The Good Captain said that many who made the trip did so through Indenture. They contracted with the Ship's Owners for free passage. In America, the Captain could sell their contracts to the highest bidder.

The agreements varied, but usually in 4 years the contracts would be fulfilled, and the immigrant was free to start his own life. Sometimes, the Proprietors of

Pennsylvania would provide them with a small piece of land for having served to build the colony. During the Indenture, the landowner was responsible to feed, clothe and house you.

Though it seemed a good prospect for making the move happen, the concept of Indenture was sour in John Cessna's mouth. Putting his sons at Indenture was not something he would be able to live with.

Mary Kate agreed with him when he shared these details with her.

"But, we have to send the boys," she stated firmly. And together they began to plan.

They had been able to save a total of £34 in the two decades of their marriage. This was buried in a pot beneath a loose stone in the hearth.

Once a month, in a very sacred, late-night ceremony, John and Mary Kate would carefully recount the treasury and add a bit more to it.

Their dream had been to one day buy a farm of their own. Mary Kate hoped to buy this one. But as they worked harder, the value of the land increased. Their own efforts were pushing the dream further away.

A new dream was born as they sifted through the well-worn coins in Mary Kate's apron. The question was simple. Should they send both or just one of the boys?

Mary dreamed of the options for a week. No combination seemed to work in her visions. Stephen and John might work against each other so much it would condemn them to failure. Alone they were sure to fail.

Her decision took a week. When it was made, it shocked her husband to his core.

"We will all go!" Mary Kate announced. Although it was more of a final pronouncement. "Neither of the boys will make it without our guidance. And if they went together, they would make a mess of it."

"You will just have to find the money," she told her husband in a quiet but firm voice. And following the supper that evening she made her announcement to her sons.

The boys were instantly excited. The adventure provoked fantastic images in their young minds. Neither of them loved this land more than he loved the possibilities that the New World offered.

John Cessna Sr. on the other hand, looked at the overwhelming task of raising the money. It was a daunting goal. They would need to raise another £26 in five months. It had taken 25 years to save the £34 they had.

And £60 would only be enough to cover the passage. They needed even more to start a new life.

John would never have bothered counting the money or making any plans if he had known the secret Mary Kathleen Cessna was keeping from him.

She dared not tell him, because it would ruin all of her dreams for her sons.

CHAPTER NINE
The Going

Captain Cowman had very few options when it came to negotiating price for passage. His ship was a business.

Everything was based on space and weight. If he carried a 150 lb. person with 50 lbs. of baggage; that was 200 lbs. of marketable cargo he would not have room for. The price was based on what profit that amount of weight and space on a ship ought to earn.

John Cessna Sr. had to raise the entire £60. He had less than six months. It was Mary Kate who pointed out to him that they would also need money at the end of the journey. The goal was raised beyond the boat fare.

They still had the option of contracting with the captain to be auctioned in America for indentured service. This was becoming more common as despair settled into the hearts of those living on rented Irish land. The need for labor, both skilled and unskilled in America was driving up the value of the contracts. But there was a caveat.

Cessna learned that if the fare were £15 in advance, it could be different at the end of the journey. If your contract were auctioned for £20, that is what you would have to repay through years of service.

So, the Cessna family began to scrimp and scrape for money. Every possible scheme was employed. Every member of the family embraced the goal with passion.

Produce from the garden which normally might have been stored for the winter, was carried to the Market on Wednesdays and Saturday. County markets were held in central locations, not for convenience of shoppers, but for convenience of the tax collectors who skimmed a share of all sales.

John Sr. was handed a blow when he approached the mill about an advance purchase of his summer crop of oats.

Landlords in London had anticipated that tenants might try to sell their crops and leave rather than pay the higher rents. Because the rents were due at the end of the year, they placed liens on all the crops, and none could be sold without landlords collecting first.

The local Magistrates (all members of the Anglican Church) were enthusiastic in their support of this new law.

John Cessna's main cash crop was unavailable to him.

Stephen and John Jr caught fish and sold them to the local pub. Before, they had exchanged these for drink, now they brought home a few pennies each time.

The three men cut and hauled thatch to the city. They hired out their labor to any farmer who might have a bit of coin to pay them. They sold most of the ducks.

The scheme which helped the most was Mary Kate's idea for the pigs. Normally, they sold the young pigs when they reached about 50lbs. These were raised and slaughtered by another farmer who could afford to feed them to maturity.

The Cessna farm just did not have enough excess food to raise a dozen piglets to full market value. That is, as Mary Kate pointed out, in a normal year they did not.

At her suggestion, all the piglets were kept. They would be raised on whatever food the family might find. If they did not plan to be there in the Fall; then the garden produce did not need to be ripe before it could be fed to the pigs.

When Spring came, the hogs would all be traded to the butcher in exchange for a dozen small kegs of salt pork.

Captain Cowman had agreed to accept this amount of stored meat in exchange for one fare of passage. It would help him feed his crew on the voyage.

The pigs ate everything. They ate every bit of green scrap from the garden. They ate cattails that the boys brought from the river. They ate weeds and wildflowers mowed from the ditches. They ate wild roots and berries. They ate every fish which was not fit for table food. They ate faster than the Cessna boys could gather something for them to eat.

The first week of April, a butcher in Belfast kept his word and converted the herd into 12 kegs of salted pork. The remainder of the meat was his to sell.

The last thing the family sold was the horse. "Marie" was the filly born of Claudine after that first Winter in Lurgan County. She had born several foals of her own. All of those had been sold through the years.

Now her faithful old soul would provide the last few coins needed for the trip.

Their packing had to be schemed just as carefully as the fundraising. Only one change of clothes each was included. All the farm tools had their handles removed and only the metal parts packed. New handles would be fashioned from the trees in America.

The most difficult choices were what to take in their ship store. It had to be small enough to fit in a water-tight box. It had to weigh no more than Captain Cowman would allow.

Yet it had to be enough of everything to last their family for the six to eight week trip to America. That is a long time to eat only food stored in a box.

Assembled in smaller packets and tucked in among the larger items were packets of garden seeds, flax seed, herbs, spices, and teas. Smaller kitchen tools and pots were wedged into three sea chests in any manner possible.

John insisted on a small keg of apples for the family to eat on the journey. His intention was that every seed would be saved to start a new orchard at journey's end. And this keg provided his own personal place to sit on the journey.

They began to feel that they were ready for the journey. But John Cessna was about to be handed news which would change everything.

For weeks, Mary Kate seemed to be growing weaker. Her cough grew deeper and raspier.

John Cessna became so alarmed that he threatened to cancel the trip and wait another year.

It was the day he returned from selling the hogs that his wife gave him the secret she had been hiding for months. The doctor had found a noise in her lungs. It meant a growth.

It had been secretly growing inside her since November. Mary Kate had known it at Christmas time, but had kept it from her husband.

With tears in her eyes, she explained why she would not be able to make the trip to America. With a firmness he had never seen, his wife explained why John and the boys must go.

John argued with his wife for two days. In both French and English he insisted that his love for her would not let him leave her behind. The boys could wait a year.

With pleading tears, Mary Kate, begged him to go. In her heart, she knew that something might come up to change their mind again. If she were not there to push them, they would never have the courage.

There would always be an excuse to keep them from fulfilling her dream. It was her dying wish that they would go.

John hid himself and cried the first day he heard her story. He spent the second day in a silent rage. He hid it from his wife, but when out of her sight he was not a man to be spoken to.

Finally, his anger gave way to an uneasy peace.

Once again, his wife was right. Once again he had to submit to her wisdom.

With a broken heart, John made a promise he did not intend to keep. At least he would not keep it as long as his wife still had breath in her body.

As if knowing his courage to leave might fail him, Mary Kate gave up her spirit just two weeks after telling her husband.

The three Cessna men buried her next to her son William and the two children who had never made it through birth.

There was no longer reason for John Cessna to stay in this stone cottage. It was an even more bitter place with her gone.

With her last bit of strength, Mary Kate had ordained a new direction for her husband and sons.

They were reluctant to leave, but committed to the dream of the woman who had brought so much singing and laughter into their lives.

By May 6th, they were ready. Captain Cowman and the ship were ready, filled to the brim with people, baggage, livestock, and marketable goods.

Culbertsons, Kirkpatricks, Campbells, Duncans and O'Neals were among the 160 immigrants on board the ship. All prayed for clear weather. The lack of it might thwart their dreams.

These families had coordinated their efforts as much as possible. They alerted one another to opportunities to earn cash.

The men even plotted how they could share tools. Culbertson was taking the tools required for building a house and Dunlap was taking the tools for carpentry and furniture building. Each family knew they could rely on the next for help with whatever need might arise.

These families from Lurgan County would form the nucleus of a co-op that would help them establish lives in Pennsylvania.

Past grievances and jealousies were forgotten by these men. As they climbed aboard Captain Cowman's ship, a rush of forgiveness was released. They stepped on deck as new men.

All the strain and pain were instantly forgotten; replaced with the intoxication of adventure and a limitless dream for the future.

In that moment, the Cessna men forgot their abuses of each other, and fell in love once again.

It is impossible to describe the bond which formed between the boys and their father as they stared out on the watery horizon. No childish blows were ever again exchanged between Stephen and John, Jr.

They had become men. Forever they would be loyal friends, even in angry disagreement.

Jean began to feel more confident in Mary Kate's dream as soon as the anchor was hauled in. The ship moved beneath their feet as though it were alive. It was as if a great beast was carrying them over the vast sea.

CHAPTER TEN
The Sea!

The first two weeks at sea were spent in dispute as to who was the sickest. Jean, having experienced sea travel times before, seemed to adjust quicker than the others.

Campbell swore that his daily breakfast of whiskey made his world dance a lot anyway, so he proudly denied any disorientation. But the foul dribbles down his waistcoat belied his superior attitude. His wife and children were sick enough for him.

The cramped quarters were not much worse than spending the nine weeks of winter huddled in tiny cottages with too many children. Eventually, everyone adjusted to sea travel and a somewhat normal life was resumed.

But normal was having 60 of your neighbors and friends, and at least 100 strangers, crammed into tiny rooms below deck. People slept on the floor or in hammocks that were strung in a spider like maze from the walls to the center posts.

It was impossible to make a nocturnal exit through the crowd without stepping on someone, or being knocked off your feet by a body swinging freely in its tethered cocoon.

The men spent much of the day on deck. The women however, stayed in the stagnant air of the ships holds. They fretted over the details of the children's lives. They kept a worried lookout for any signs of sickness. Of course, they blamed their husbands for every inconvenience and anything lacking on the journey.

None of them spoke of their hunger or the inadequate quality of food they had to eat and share. They only talked about the inconsequential problems.

They ignored the issues which threatened to take the lives of some of their party. Starvation, cold, sickness ... those topics were left for each one to discuss with their Creator, in the quiet corners of his or her mind.

Each day morphed into the next. It was impossible to tell if they were making suitable time or if they were behind schedule. Captain Cowman was optimistic, but they could see that he did not know for sure.

The men spent the day talking in minute detail about what needed to be done in the new land. They debated over which seeds to plant first. They proposed a variety of shelters they might build.

They cajoled about who was catching the most grief from their wives and children. They masked their fears behind braggadocio and good-natured criticism.

The boys plied the sailors for information about the new country they were coming to. For a brief period, Stephen Cessna even thought he might like a life at sea.

Then the storm hit.

Three days of pitching waves, cutting wind and

icy rain. None could sleep or eat. Only the captain seemed happy. At least it was pushing them in the right direction.

The captain kept the ship running before the wind. On a normal day, he would have to lay out a zig-zag course so the ship could catch enough wind to push it mostly in the right direction. With this storm, he could keep the vessel in a straight line to the West.

It tossed the passengers around in an erratic pattern. There were periods when the ship settled into a predictable routine of rising and lowering with the waves. But the distance between the peak and the valley was more than thirty feet, even at midship.

The passengers and crew soon learned the rhythm and could move about reasonably well. It was an interesting dance, trying to anticipate the movement of the floor with every step.

In the middle of one night, Jean Cesna had had enough of hiding below decks. He was feeling claustrophobic and needed air.

The inexorable storm had caused him to doubt his choices again. Again, he worried that he had made a mistake in bringing the boys on this trip.

He had spent the long hours of the storm reliving the regrets of his life. He remembered the fair lands of his home in Normandie. He could almost taste the sweet wines of his homeland, and feel the warm sun on his face as he had wandered the pastures.

In his mind, he returned to being Jean le Cesne of

his youth. His memories and dreams were in French.

For some reason he could remember one old milk cow the family owned, Claudette. *Funny,* he thought. *We probably had 20 cows, but she is the only one I remember.*

He could not make himself recall the face of his father, only the voice. This saddened him greatly.

Lying in his hammock in the cold and dark, his mind revisited all of the days he spent as a soldier. The faces of those who died in sickness and battle came back to him, but not the names.

In one dream his bride came to him and revived their wedding day. He re-experienced the feeling of holding newborn William in his hands. Four funerals washed over his memory, as did long hard days of struggling against the soil.

Mostly Jean remembered all the frigid days of his life. That was what woke him up. The cold! He was cold! He hated it.

Maybe if he could get up and move around he would not feel it in his old bones so much. Swinging out of his canvas bed, he gingerly made his way between the swinging bodies of his fellow passengers. He headed for the steps to the wheelhouse. Slowly he climbed them in the periods between the ship's sudden shifts up or down.

A ship tossed in the storm is always unpredictable, to say the least.

As he neared the top of the incline, the ship made a quick lurch of about 15 feet to starboard. Jean's 60-

year-old body was suddenly flying through the dark.

His body wrapped itself around one of the central pillars with a sickening thud. It had struck two or three people in its brief flight. They began a chorus of complaints.

Jean moaned a ghastly sound. Soon, many in the room were stirring, and others were lighting lanterns.

Stephen and John noticed that their father was missing from his hammock and began to move towards the commotion. The lump of humanity on the floor looked nothing like their father.

Not knowing what else to do, they retrieved his broken body and returned it to his bunk. Jean screamed in pain wherever they tried to hold him. He was beyond conversation and spent the remaining hours until daylight, keeping them all awake with his moaning.

No one in the group could mistake the fatal tone of his groans. The brothers lay awake in the dark worrying about their father.

At first light, the damage was obvious. His body had wrapped itself around the pier, crushing his liver. Black clouds were developing under the skin around his entire mid-section. He was bleeding internally.

Death was certain.

Jean felt somehow at peace, knowing that his fight was nearly over. He began to thank his God for what blessings he had known.

Jean thought it appropriate that he would remain with the sea. He had not had a home in a long time.

He felt it imperative that the boys go on and complete the dream ... his dream. Looking at his two grown sons, he struggled with his final directives.

"Go! Plant our family in America. Maybe one day you can go back to France," he whispered to them. "You will feel at home there. You have roots there. But look out for each other in America."

In the end, his brain was so starved for oxygen that Jean simply fell asleep. By noon he had been sewn into his canvas hammock and all were gathered on deck to bid him farewell.

The storm had faded at about the same time as his life.

Although familiar with the harsh terms of life and death, John and Stephen were in shock for several days. They had come on this trip because their mother had made them promise. Had it not been for their father's stubborn nature they might have quit the dream. They had obeyed without question.

Now they had to decide which direction they wanted for themselves. In the end, they decided to trust his choice for them, and see what happened. He had wanted the family to rebuild itself in a better place. They would go on.

As the storm faded, a sense of hubris fell over the crowd. Most were surprised that they had survived.

For several of the passengers, their faith returned. They were now more confident than ever, that God was giving his blessing on their quest.

For two brothers, the burden of losing their father refused to lessen. He had been their guide. He had been the force which told them what their next move should be.

Until that morning after the storm, their parents had made every decision for them. Now they were on their own.

The competitive relationship between Stephen (26) and John (18) was washed away by the storm. John would now look to his older brother for direction. Stephen now assumed the role of head of the house.

CHAPTER ELEVEN
A New World

The storm had shortened the trip by about a week.

On Sunay, June 12, 1718, six weeks to the day from their departure, the ship entered Delaware Bay. The rails of the ship were lined with eager and cautious faces.

The sons of John and Mary Kate Cessna carefully studied their new world.

They saw mostly forests. The few settled areas they spotted were separated by miles and miles of wild woodlands.

The land was lush and green. It was teeming with life of every description: fish jumping from the surf, deer and strange creatures grazing along the shore, birds of every kind filling the sky around them.

On occasion, they even caught a glimpse of one of the tribal peoples. But it was never more than a glimpse. By the time you could call others to look, they were gone.

They could see an endless sea of trees. There was little land ready to farm in the way they were accustomed to. In Ireland they had to dig stone from the soil. Here they would have removed the roots of massive trees.

Those who had chosen to pay their passage with labor, began to be grateful for their choice. No one had any idea where or how to begin a life in this world. Indentured service guaranteed them a place to start, a shelter to sleep in, and a meal at the end of each day.

The cost of docking in Philadelphia had grown to exorbitant levels. To save money for the ship's owners, Captain Cowman had docked 30 miles distant from the capital. New Castle was quickly becoming an efficient harbor.

The Captain explained that they had stopped short of Philadelphia because taxes and docking fees had grown too high in that city. New Castle was a much friendlier place to land.

The process of becoming servants was much simpler than any had imagined. Men and women stayed on the ship until a contract was made; but could wander around the port of New Castle at will.

Captain Cowman placed an ad in a Philadelphia paper, listing the number of persons and what skills they brought. Employers came to the ship from all over the province and interviewed the candidates.

Those accepting servitude were given explanation of Pennsylvania Laws for Indentured Service by Captain Cowman. Each was given a clear date of when their service would end, and the benefits they could expect while serving.

They had to give 10 to 12 hours labor per day; were not allowed to leave without permission; and the Quaker community would not tolerate cruelty of either slave or servant.

It was clear that each employer expected to profit handsomely from their service. Their labor would be hard.

The ship which docked next to Captain Cowman's carried a load of Blacks from one of the Spanish colonies. The Europeans were immediately curious.

The reception for the slaves was much different than that of the Scotch and Irish. The Quakers had no qualms about slavery, but frowned on the cruelty which was given to the blacks.

The indentured servants from Ireland were cheaper and could speak English, and so were purchased before the slaves.

In a week's time, nearly all the ship's passengers had been given a position and destination.

The Cessna brothers were among the last. They were not sacrificing their freedom after such a long struggle. While Stephen and his little brother John were at a loss for what to do next, selling themselves into indenture they did not want.

Their father would never have wanted that. But what should they do next? They did not have enough money to buy land. They barely had enough to feed themselves, and that would not last for long.

Together, the brothers wandered the town of New Castle searching for what they should do next. Stephen was certain that God would give them a direction.

Each night they returned to sleep on Captain Cowman's ship. Long into the dark they talked of what they must do next.

They wandered the town trying to gather what opportunities might exist. There were many. Most of those were undesirable to Stephen's independent nature.

On their eighth day in port, John Cessna met Ashman Stedham. The two men liked each other from the beginning. Both were direct and knew what they wanted. Each was straight spoken with no hidden meanings in their declarations.

Stedham had inherited land from his father, Dr. Tymen Stedham. He owned an exceptionally large section of land located between the Christiana River and

Brandywine Creek.

In fact, he owned the lion's share of Christiana Hundred. And he was looking for ways to make a profit from his estate.

The Cessna's had always rented. The family managed the King's land in France. Their father had rented in Ireland. It was the arrangement which made the two brothers the most comfortable. It was the arrangement which made them feel most free.

The land they discussed was situated between New Castle and Philadelphia; 10 miles from the port and 20 miles from the capital. The new King's Road cut through the property and assured that there would always be commercial traffic near at hand.

Ashman Stedham surveyed the two brothers. They appeared strong and eager for arduous work. He had lots of work to offer them. Stephen and John Cessna began their lives in America not as indentured servants, but as hired hands for Ashmun Steadham. The work consisted of clearing timber and caring for livestock.

CHAPTER TWELVE
The Time Had Come

After two years, the brothers began to grow restless from living in the shack their employer had provided. It had taken a full two years for them to feel comfortable in the new land.

It had also taken that long before they had saved enough money to strike out on their own.

Something dramatic made a change in their dreams.

Stephen Cessna met a young woman at the weekly market. She completely stole his heart. Patience French was captivating beyond any woman he had ever met. Her red hair had drawn him to her like a moth is drawn to a flame. (We do not know her true last name.)

The need was irresistible. He knew he must convince her to spend the rest of her life with him.

But he had no home to offer her.

Approaching his employer, Stephen convinced Stedham to rent him a five acre parcel of land. It was not much, but it was all that Cessna could afford. A rent of just £2 seems a great challenge considering how small his wages had been up until that point.

Pooling their money and working every hour they could get free; the two brothers built a hewn log house on the land. And Stephen made his offer to the woman of his dreams.

Stephen pursued Patience with a fierce passion. He became quite a comical spectacle in their community as he sought to convince her and everyone else of his love.

Of the brothers, Stephen was always the most reactionary. John was the more cautious and calculating.

In 1721, Patience French married Stephen Cessna and moved into the house along Brandywine Creek. The brother, John, would live with them for a while as well.

Soon, John had found a new career which took him away from the house for days at a time. He began to work on the docks at New Castle, helping freighters load their wagons. Eventually, he drove one of the wagons all the way to Philadelphia, or sometimes up to Kennett.

The first Cessna child born in the New World was John, born to Patience at her parent's home in 1722. The child's father was away on a trading trip.

John French was quick to introduce his son-in-law to the business of hauling goods for trading with the Indians.

The small Cessna plantation along Kennett Road became a prosperous place. To the East, their property was bounded by Brandywine Creek. On the South, it bordered the land of Daniel Few, a blacksmith. Later, the Few family built a mill along Brandywine Creek. The neighborhood was growing quickly.

On the West of the Cessna property was an old Indian trail which led to the Northwest. Months after the Cessna brothers arrived, the path was widened into a road leading to Kennett, Lancaster, Harris' Ferry and beyond.

On the north, was more undeveloped property of Stedham. It ran all the way up to Rattlesnake Hill.

The home which Stephen and John built for Patience was modest but not too small. A great room of

20'x30' provided a large communal area for living. Over time, three smaller rooms for sleeping were added to the back wall, each about 8'x 9'.

Neighbors began to locate around them. Some of them had daughters. The initial stages of the town of Wilmington formed just a mile to their South.

Life was still hard and challenging. Everything they needed had to be built or earned from nothing. But this new land did not deny them a reward for their labors.

John Cessna was drawn to a quiet beauty named Rachel. His approach was more deliberate and determined. He spent three years "selling" her on the brilliance of his detailed plans for their future.

For her part, Rachael did not need three years' worth of deliberate planning. She was ready to marry the moment she looked into John Cessna's pale blue eyes.

They married at Christmas in 1724, and moved into a newly added bedroom at his brother's home. Their son "John, Jr." was born there on 26 January 1726.

The first two Cessna sons born in America were named for the old Frenchman.

Two years later, Rachel's daughter Mary was born. In those early years, it was just more economical for the two families to share one household. The two men seemed to be always traveling, anyway.

The two wives, Patience and Rachel not only provided each other with company, but with help in childrearing.

CHAPTER THIRTEEN
Two Paths for Two Brothers

The primary economic driver for New Castle county was transportation. What was unloaded at the docks was destined for the people living in the interior. And what was being shipped back to England came from the interior.

From the docks at New Castle, cargo which was marked for specific businesses and individuals was loaded onto wagons, and transported 30 miles to Philadelphia. Traffic used the newly built King's Road. Those wagons would then pass by Stephen Cessna's home.

A portion of the cargo had been brought by the Captain on speculation; to sell to whomever. This was sold on the docks at New Castle. Each time a new ship arrived; buyers came from Philadelphia to take advantage of what was available.

The King's Road, and the road following Brandywine Creek up to Kennett, were heavily traveled in 1720. Wagon, horse, and foot traffic kept the road continually busy. Stephen and Patience Cessna lived along the superhighway of their day.

All of this cargo needed to be moved by local labor, using local wagons and horses. Unloading cargo, and transporting it to a market were quick ways for men to make copper and silver coins.

A good part of the freight being hauled was not bound for Philadelphia, but to the forests of the interior. Its purpose was for trading with the Indians.

Ambitious men had traveled far into the forest to trade with the native peoples. They built remote cabins which served as trading posts. They returned with large bundles of animal furs and pelts. These were sold to ship captains for transport to markets in England.

John French introduced Stephen and John Cessna to the business of hauling freight for the traders.

He brought his new son into the business of carrying things to be sold to the Indians. They returned with furs and other goods which would be sold in England.

In 1720 there were no roads past Kennett, only harness paths. Each wagon's cargo had to be reloaded onto pack horses. While a wagon might carry 1-2 tons of freight, one horse could only carry 200-400 pounds. It might take 10 or more horses to carry what one wagon could carry.

All of this required hiring local men to load/unload and guide pack trains into the forest.

The same freighters who carried these items to trading posts deep into the forest, then carried back items which were many times more valuable to Europeans.

The most lucrative way for a man to make a living in 1720 was to work with freight. It took a great deal of man hours to keep wagons and horse-pack trains moving smoothly up and down the road; a road that ran right in front of the Cessna home.

It was obvious to the Cessna brothers that the best money lay in working with freight.

After the birth of his son and daughter, John Cessna gained a new passion to build a secure future. He joined his brother in hauling trade goods into the forest.

Eight years after hearing the letter read in Culbertson's Pub, Stephen and John Cessna were fully a part of the new world.

The heart and dreams of the old French warrior still beat in their souls.

Stephen and Patience soon had three sons. John Cessna was born in 1723, Stephen Jr born in 1724, and Thomas born in 1726.

With the birth of John Cessna Jr, to John and Rachel in January 1726, the Cessna Clan in America now numbered eight souls.

CHAPTER FOURTEEN
The Indians

Because they often wandered far from their home, it was not long before Stephen and John saw their first Indian. They appeared in almost any location, with the startle and surprise of ghosts.

Though they had bargained with the English for Europeans to settle in this region, the natives still felt the right to wander it at will.

For the Colony's first 70 years, whites and Indians were able to live alongside each other in relative peace. Though there were isolated problems and disagreements, they managed to tolerate the extreme differences in their lifestyles. They even profited from the relationship.

It was not at all unusual for one of the newcomers to be working in some gainful enterprise, and suddenly discover he was being carefully studied by a silent apparition of a "savage." They appeared and disappeared with an unnerving ability.

Sometimes one of the Cessna brothers might see a face in the foliage. Sometimes they encountered a painted man who was like an iconic figure that would one day become the cigar store wooden Indian. They stood openly and motionlessly in public, watching the comings and goings of these strange and noisy people.

Wherever they went, whatever their business, for Stephen and John Cessna, it seemed that the red man was a predictable backdrop for life.

John Cessna knew the natives were highly spiritual. He had seen one warrior make a pilgrimage to the summit of a mountain and engage in solitary worship. Before a small and smoky fire, he offered his thanks for life's blessings and sought guidance for the future. His fire was a signal for the creator, but it was noted by all of the white settlers in the valley.

The native's silhouette against the sky was visible to English settlers in the valleys on both sides of the mountain.

As far as John Cessna was concerned, this warrior was making a clear statement. "I am grateful for what Manito has given me." But the subliminal message which the newcomers received was, *This is still my land.*

The cultural differences between the races were startling. The concepts of ownership of the land and personal property were vastly different for the red man. One thing which is often overlooked is their extreme generosity in hospitality.

It was customary for them to freely share all they had so that none in the village had need. It was common for an Indian to simply walk into the home of another, expecting to be fed, sheltered, and given an unquestioned share of whatever bounty had befallen the family.

Once an Indian just walked through the door of the Cessna house, unannounced and uninvited. Stephen and John had a tough time convincing their wives that the man had not been a threat. Thankfully, he had left quietly when the women began to scream and throw things at him. It was a tense encounter.

The warrior/hunter felt it his duty to provide for others. He would sooner lie down naked and hungry in the snow than believe he had been lax in his duties of hospitality. When one prospered, the entire village prospered.

Blessings were freely passed through the hands of the "family." If a white man presented a gift to a brave (be it a gun or a string of beads), it might pass through two dozen hands before it "stuck."

Such behavior was not only new, but incomprehensible to the white man. Communication between the races, and assigning value to things, was difficult to say the least.

In early July of 1721, John French came to Stephen with a new assignment. The governor himself was taking a large expedition to the Indian town of Conestoga.

French had been contracted to transport a goodly amount of trade supplies. Another company had been hired to carry the food and equipment needed by the Governor's entourage. It was to be an unusually large pack train.

At the government warehouse, Stephen and his fellow teamsters picked up the largest load of trade goods they had ever seen. Reviewing the invoice, Stephen was amazed at the wealth of their cargo. He was asked to sign a receipt for the following:

"500 pounds of powder, 600 pounds of lead, 45 guns, 100 blankets, 200 yards of cloth, 100 shirts, 40 hats, 40 pairs of shoes and buckles, 40 pairs of stockings, 100 hatchets, 500 knives, 100 hoes, 100 tobacco tongs, 100 scissors, 500 awls, 120 combs 2000 needles, 1000 flints, 20 looking glasses, 2 pounds of Vermillion, 100 tin pots, 25 gallons of rum, 200 pounds of tobacco, 1000 pipes, and 24 dozens of garter."

Assuming that these would be used to purchase furs, he protested that they did not have enough wagons and animals to return with such a bounty. Stephen was told in abrupt terms that these were payment for a land purchase negotiated by the governor years earlier.

Then he was given his biggest surprise.

As they were leaving, the quartermaster had them stop by the armory. Each man was given a fire lock musket and five rounds of ammunition. The governor was taking armed militia with him. Every man in this expedition was to be armed.

Stephen protested he had never even held a gun, let alone learned to fire one. He was told not to worry.

"Just carry the thing and try to look fierce. If the shooting starts, give this to someone who knows how to use it and start running."

He thought it was a very rude and abrupt answer.

Now he began to worry deeply about what challenges this trip might bring.

On July 5, 1721, Governor Keith led a force of seventy armed horsemen and a train of trade goods to treat with the Indians at Conestoga. Not only were all of the Conestoga chiefs in attendance, but also four delegates of the five Iroquois tribes.

The "people of the Long House" had long ago banded together in a mighty alliance and made all of the tribes in Pennsylvania subject to them. All land deals and negotiations had to be completed with Iroquois permission.

And the four delegates brought with them 100 warriors to help carry home their share of the bounty. Stephen Cessna was overwhelmed at the spectacle.

Savage-looking faces were everywhere, and they wandered at will among the Englishmen. His mind raced with every horrible atrocity he had ever heard repeated.

Cessna hoped to make himself invisible to the natives by remaining in a cluster of teamsters. But an occasional brave would simply stroll to the group and study them in a deliberate and intimidating manner.

One of the warriors stopped inches from Cessna's face and began a deathly stare.

"Mon Dieu!" exhaled Stephen. "What is he looking at?" he asked of the man next to him.

"He is looking to see if he can smell fear on any of us," the man whispered. "Try to look like the Devil's own man. Do not blink or look him in the eye. Just stand still and pretend he is invisible."

Some men were bold enough to exchange tokens with the warriors who glided silently among their ranks. In complete terror, Stephen chose to remain frozen, pretending he could not even see them.

When he thought no one could hear, he muttered French curses under his breath.

Each of the savages was a unique work of art. The color of their clothing, weapons and tattoos was startling. The elaborate effort made by each of them to look more ferocious than the next was unbelievable.

While the white men copied fashion from each other, it was individualism which ruled the Indian decoration.

It was the worst period of waiting Stephen had ever endured. His brain was overloaded with the sights, smells, and sounds of that day. It was certainly more drama in just one spin around the planet than he had expected to find in a lifetime.

Sleep would totally escape him that night.

He was told that the Governor was negotiating some kind of peace. The Iroquois were staging punishment raids on the tribes in the south. They were traversing the same valleys and waterways that they had for years on their path to war.

The problem was that these lands were now inhabited by whites, who were brought to panic at the sight of war parties. The governor was successful in getting them to change their route and thus preserved peace between the races … for this season anyway.

The party returned home in triumph and everyone was happy, except Stephen. For the first time, he understood the might of the red man.

His next purchase was for his own gun, to replace the one loaned to him by the government for that trip. He learned to use it. It would be his constant companion anytime he headed to the back country.

The older of the Cessna brothers could still see that prosperity lay down that trail into the Wilderness. Jeopardy, prosperity, and fortune all waited in abundance for the courageous soul who would endeavor.

CHAPTER FIFTEEN
Land

In the early 1730's, life offered a new opportunity for the Cessna men.

The Penn family, proprietors, and landlords of the Pennsylvania Colony, were generous about making land available to newcomers. The process was affordable and inviting.

Persons wishing to move into the wilderness and establish a plantation only had to apply for a license and pay a small fee. The license was for a specific number of acres, which they were free to choose from in any location within the boundaries of a designated territory.

It was first come-first served, as to the quality of the land. But the Penns were careful about not issuing licenses in areas that had not been clearly purchased from the Indians by treaty.

The settler then had several years to make improvements to the land and define the bounds of his property with various means. He was required to pay "quit rents" until he was ready to patent the land.

It usually took about five to 10 years to carve a plantation from virgin forests, depending on how many people shared the labor. At that point, the farmer could apply for a warrant.

This was done at the land office in Lancaster. The warrant was a request for an official survey and eventually patenting the land. This last step meant complete ownership. At that point you stopped paying rent and began paying taxes to the government.

Since arriving in America, the Cessna brothers frequently heard the phrase, "wealth is in the land."

Brother, John Cessna, took the advice to heart and kept a constant eye to expand his future.

In 1734, Samuel Blunston was authorized by the Penn Family to begin issuing licenses for land on the west side of the Susquehanna River.

On the 19th of July 1734, John Cessna was among the very first men to apply for a license to take up 200 acres on the West side of the Susquehanna River.

His purchase is recorded in Blunston's Book of Licenses. He chose a spot along the South side of the Conewago Creek, about a mile from where it joined the Susquehanna River. It was surrounded by wilderness.

John did live and work on this property for a few years. On 26 October 1737, he completed a warrant application and requested to have it surveyed by a government official. To apply for this survey, he had to have lived on the land to make improvements.

In 1737 that disaster struck!

John, Rachel, 10 year son, John, Jr. and six year old Mary, began to improve the property west of the large river. He had finished a cabin when tragedy struck.

The Penn family had purchased this land from the Iroquois. But the Delaware had not agreed to the sale. The natives still considered it their land, and were surprised when they found a white family settling in.

On a bright summer day, John was away from the cabin clearing brush from a new field. He was teaching his son the proper way to use an axe. Rachel and Mary were in the cabin.

The door and windows were open to provide relief from the heat.

A lone Indian wandered into the farmstead and was surprised to see whites living here.

The Delaware brave casually entered the cabin to investigate the newcomers.

He probably meant no threat, but when he suddenly appeared between Rachel and her daughter, the young mother was terrified.

She completely panicked. Striking a feeble first blow, the young girl fled the house and ran for her husband.

In her confusion she ran in the wrong direction, taking her in the opposite direction of her help.

The curious warrior slowly followed, confused by her reaction. He could not understand why the woman was running from him.

Seeing the man following her, Rachel ran even harder. She was almost blinded by her fear.

Reaching the river, and seeing the wild looking man close behind her, Rachel threw herself in the water and tried the impossible. In panic, she gave her life in an effort to swim the wide and swift river.

Still bewildered as to her erratic and inhospitable behavior, the Delaware brave retrieved her body and carried it back to the cabin. He was still there holding the little girl with great gentleness when John returned.

The tragedy left John with two small children, an unfinished home, and no desire to care for either.

Patience insisted that he return to their home. She and Stephen had just purchased a house on second street in Wilmington. Patience now assumed the mothering responsibilities for John Jr. and Mary.

The younger of the two brothers would be lost in grief for two years. John cherished the land he and Rachel had chosen. But he could not bring himself to resume its development. The warrant lay unused for decades.

On his death bed, in 1796, John Cessna listed the properties he had claimed and developed through the decades. He carefully described the location of the land he had gotten through a Blunston License.

He could never bring himself to sell it, or finish it. It became a wilderness shrine to the wife of his youth. It was her resting place.

Stephen and John Cessna almost never worked together on any of their trips of hauling freight. Stephen spent a great deal of time carrying trade goods to remote places far into the interior. John worked mostly in hauling merchandise from New Castle to Philadelphia, Lancaster, or other towns. But on occasion their paths did happen to cross.

That is what happened one day in March of 1739. With the snows melting early, more transportation was happening. The brothers crossed paths at McGee's Tavern in Lancaster.

McGee's was a favorite for those men who had immigrated from Ireland. Most of the taverns in Pennsylvania served German style beer. McGee's was one of the few places one could by a good Irish Black Stout.

John spotted his brother the moment he walked into the place. Stephen was sitting at a corner table, staring into his drink, and looking as though he was seeing the end of life.

"Now, what can be so bad that it has you looking like Aunt Sally's cow, Big Brother."

Stephen looked up in surprise. Then a grin filled his face.

"You have a more intimate acquaintance with Aunt Sally's cow than I do, little brother."

They laughed and exchanged loving insults as brothers do. When John had a beer in front of him, Stephen was ready to talk.

"I am so tired of sleeping on the ground, little brother. I am tired of not being home to watch my kids grow, and torment the Mrs.

"I need to find work that keeps me off the road. I am 46 years old, for Christ's sake." Stephen finished.

John took a deep breath. "I have been feeling the same thing. Agnes says that a man is not supposed to go wandering down the highway when he has a new wife, especially when she is pregnant.

John Cessna had just taken a second wife, Agnes Campbell, daughter of his father's friend. She was immediately unhappy with his traveling career. Stephen's remark had reminded him that he was now 40 years old himself.

"But what can I do? I have to make a living. I put all of my savings into that place on Conewago Creek. I can't afford to buy another."

"I know what you mean. Wilmington is getting too crowded, and too expensive. Patience and I spent our entire savings on that house on Second Street. And it is already too small for us.

"Besides" Stephen continued. "Wilmington is getting too civilized for me."

"I was thinking the same thing. Last time I was there I saw the new jail they had built."

"Jail?!" interjected Stephen. "It looks more like a cage to me. They are already throwing debtors into it. Yes, civilization has certainly arrived."

Sipping at their beer, the Cessna brothers continued to grouse and complain.

Each was unhappy with their hometown. Each was worn down from the wandering life. Each of them had been thinking the same things on their own. It was one of the few times in their lives when the brothers were in agreement.

Stephen Cessna went first. "I have a mind to sell the place in town and take up a land warrant in the country. I think I can get just enough out of the house to make it happen."

"Really?" asked John. "How much will it take? Where would you go?" His curiosity peaked. He had been looking at similar options.

"For £15 I can get a warrant for two hundred acres. I have gotten a place picked out." Stephen's voice was growing excited. This was the first time he had spoken the plan aloud to anyone.

"I will need another £6-8 for the tools to build a new house. And I think I will have that much saved after this trip."

John grinned back at his brother. He was immediately excited for him. And he was also envious. "I wish I was as ready as you." John said. "All my savings are gone. I could not move if I wanted to. Agnes isn't about to move with the baby coming.

"But if you and Patience sell, we will HAVE to find a new place."

Stephen looked at his brother and took a deep breath. "I have been thinking about your situation, little brother. I think there might be a way.

"You remember when Edward Shippen was talking about starting his own land company?"

John Cessna took a long sip and nodded his head.

"Well, he is buying a couple thousand acres at the place where the trading path splits up into several trails leading over the mountains. He is already calling it Shippen's Farm."

John interrupted him, "But I haven't got enough money to buy a warrant from the land office, and surely not enough to buy some from Shippen!"

"That is the best part," Stephen continued. "Shippen weren't planning to sell any of that land. He wants to rent it. It will not take any money up front. He already has about fifteen families from Wilmington signed up."

John was suddenly extremely interested. "No money up front? How…?"

"You rent with a promise to own. No money down."

Now John looked dejected. "I am not ready for no more farm in the wilderness. The last one nearly killed me, and did kill Rachael. Besides, Agnes wouldn't have a part of it."

Stephen smiled big. He knew this would be the reaction of his younger brother. "You haven't heard the best part. Shippen is laying out a whole new town. And he is leasing out the town lots the same as the farms...no money up front."

"You mean..." John stuttered.

"Yup. You just need to have enough money to move yourself and build a cabin. You can be right in the middle of town if you want.

"Widow Piper just opened herself a place in the middle of where he is building the town. If she can live in the wilderness, Agnes can too."

Agnes and Jannet Piper were friends. The Campbell family had helped the Piper family get settled a few years earlier when they first arrived in Wilmington. After John Piper died, the Campbells had helped the widow and her children in a number of ways.

Agnes just might be willing.

The two brothers visited well into the wee hours of morning. Their excitement increased as they discussed the possibilities.

Stephen wanted to start a ford where all those wagons and horses would have to pay him to cross. John began to dream of having a store and possibly a tavern where teamsters could sleep warm and dry. From personal experience, he knew what they needed and what they could afford.

When Stephen walked back to his pack train, and John walked back to his wagons, their steps were lighter. They each had the beginning of a new dream. It was a dream where they would be at home every night, yet still make money from the freight being hauled up and down the Trader's Path.

CHAPTER SIXTEEN
New Opportunity

1739 brought the opportunity the Cessna brothers were waiting for. Stephen quickly assessed that the wilderness path was receiving increased traffic, and that those shipments were increasing in value. He guessed correctly that the path would become a wagon road and continue to grow in its use and importance.

Wealth moved up and down that road like salmon spawning in the fall streams. Stephen Cessna often bragged that he could hear silver and gold coins jingling in men's pockets as they passed by his home on Kennett Road.

It was a joke that always made Patience laugh. But she thought it was all idle chatter until April of 1739. Stephen Cessna announced that the family was moving.

Stephen chose 200 acres along the Wilderness Road. He chose the spot where traders crossed the

Swatara Creek, just three miles short of Harris' Trading Post, and the ferry over the Susquehanna.

He had crossed this creek enough times to know that it was a challenge. In dry weather it was a lovely place to ford.

In rainy weather, it was a muddy mire that could mean a long delay, and the chance of a horse breaking a leg. In the Winter months, it became a danger to both animal and human.

Taking a license for two hundred acres of land on the south side of the creek, Stephen began to build an all-weather ford. He and the boys spent weeks felling trees and sinking logs into gravel at the creek bottom.

It was right alongside the ford provided by the natural course of the river. But his would be usable all year round.

In this way, he intended to stop traveling with the freight, yet still profit from it passing in front of his home. Patience was delighted because it meant she would have her husband home every evening.

Although Cessna only charged a few pence for its use, it became a steady and growing source of income. The family prospered. The family grew. In 1740 Patience delivered twins, Theophilus and Thea.

John Cessna sought out Edward Shippen and asked about what opportunities might be available.

Edward Shippen was the first speculator to grab up a part of the new land being offered by the Governor.

After crossing the Susquehanna River at Harris' Ferry, the trading path entered Cumberland Valley. The valley runs northeast to southwest in a broad sweep that runs from the Susquehanna River at Harrisburg, PA all the way down to North Carolina.

South Mountain creates a beautiful basin between itself and the wild range of sharp ridges that make up the main body of the Appalachia Range. It provides a long, beautiful valley that is lush in every respect.

In Pennsylvania this paradise is known as Cumberland; in Virginia and further south, it is called Shenandoah.

Those men who had been carrying trade goods to the distant tribes, had long been admiring this valley as a future home. A number of squatters were already settled there, not waiting for government permission.

In 1737, Edward Shippen purchased two tracts of land from the Governor, totally 2400 acres. It was in the lower part of Cumberland Valley where the trading path divided to climb the mountains in various directions.

The place where the old Indian Path crossed Burd's Run was destined to become a cross-roads town known as Shippensburg. And in 1739, Shippen began to give the first leases to new settlers.

John had just married Agnes Campbell, the daughter of Will. She was 13 years younger than John, and a fellow refugee from Ireland. This union began as more of necessity than a romance.

While this alliance was not born from youthful passion, it had stronger bounds. Each shared a past, and a determined vision for a better future. And their commonality of goals created a close partnership.

John now had every reason to want his own place, and to start building his own fortune. The lure of land was great.

What John Cessna definitely did NOT want was another experience with a wilderness farm. He decided to become a town merchant. And he picked the perfect lot to open a store.

In 1739, John Cessna was one of the first people to take a 25 year lease from Edward Shippen. He chose Lot 22 which was on the main street.

It was across the Warrior's Path from the Widow Piper's Tavern. He also purchased an out lot which he could use for stables.

Widow Piper's was a two story stone building which could accommodate a dozen travelers. Those with money slept in beds on the second floor.

The teamsters and poorer travelers slept on pallets on the first floor or in the yard. Widow Piper's immediately became the center of commerce for the new village. Every important traveler enjoyed her hospitality.

Their servants, and the teamsters who hauled freight for the wealthy guests of Widow Piper, needed cheaper accommodations and meals. John and Agnes Cessna intended to target those travelers as the source of their fortunes.

When the Cessna wagon pulled up in front of the vacant field, John was filled with pride. "Here, dear wife! Here is where we start a new life."

Agness was less than impressed. But she was far too pregnant to travel even another mile.

John and Agnes settled down to raise a family. They were blessed with the arrival of Charles in 1740. Following Charles came Elizabeth, Margaret, Evans, Joseph, Jonathan, William, and James.

John Cessna, Jr. was now 14 years old. He was immediately put to work helping his father provide for a new wife and a growing flock of small children.

His stepmother was only a few years older than himself. This made their relationship more than a little awkward. It was hard for John, Jr. to accept supervision from her.

Back on Swatara Creek, the older of the Cessna brothers was having trouble with his neighbors. In 1743, Stephen joined his neighbors in petitioning the Quarter Sessions Court for improvements to the Wilderness Road.

The petition mentions Stephen's plantation and ford as a specific landmark for the road. This had the misfortune of bringing Cessna to attention of the Proprietors.

Throughout the 1740s, the Quakers of Chester and Lancaster Counties increasingly complained about the contentious social habits of the Scotts and Irish immigrants.

The Quakers were pressuring the Governor to move the unruly people West of the Susquehanna, into the Cumberland Valley. The Proprietors (Penn Family) had their land agents begin to do just that.

The Penns issued directives to offer very lucrative deals to any Scott or Irish settlers who would sell out in Lancaster, to move west of the big river. There were hints of unpleasant consequences to any who resisted.

Stephen was finally persuaded to move into the valley that his brother was helping to settle. The most readily available land was in the new community of Carlisle, just twenty miles East of his brother.

Following John's example, Stephen and Patience chose to live in town and not on an isolated farm. They purchased a house and lot near the town square.

Two of their sons, Stephen and Thomas would eventually take up farms just outside the town. In 1743, shortly after building the ford on Swatara Creek, Stephen's oldest son, John, married Pryscilla Foulke. When his parents moved from Swatara, John took his part of their profits and licensed a piece of land in York County. It was at a place where the path found a ford across the Yellow Breeches Creek.

At that place, young John Cessna began a tanning business. It was located just three miles from Harris' Ferry and less than 10 miles from Carlisle.

John and Pryscilla Foulke began to welcome the third generation of Cessna's in America. Stephen, John, and Ruth were all born to them before 1750.

In 1751, Carlisle became the county seat for Cumberland County. It soon became a community of wealthy politicians and lawyers. Stephen and Patience had chosen a home with great commercial possibilities.

Shippensburg also became a bustling and profitable community. But it had a different atmosphere than Carlise. It was now the end of the road for wagons, and the point for transferring freight to pack trains of horses.

In Shippensburg everything going West had to be loaded onto pack horses for the narrow trails. When they returned with bundles of furs, the wagons were loaded to carry the cargo back to the seaports.

At its peak, there were as many as five hundred horses in Shippensburg, more equines than people. The animals were strung together in groups of 8 to 12 with one teamster at the front and one at the rear. Each horse carried   200 to 400 pounds of merchandise and had a bell around its neck.

The tinkle and jingle of pack animal bells was constant background music for the village. When visitors complained about the racket of bells clanging all night and day, John Cessna love to pause and say, "Sounds like money to me."

And indeed almost every train of freight that came jingling down the path yielded a little coin for John Cessna's tavern. In a brief time, he opened a store.

Though not as nice as Widow Piper's, Cessna's place was more affordable. For just a little coin, men could find a hot meal, a bit of alcohol to ease his pain, and a dry place to sleep.

At one time, as many as fourteen inns operated in Shippensburg. They functioned to accommodate the professional travelers, and ranged in quality depending on their client.

Every farmer made profit by growing hay and grain to feed the voracious appetite of the four-legged visitors, and whiskey to fortify the two legged ones.

A good deal of cash flowed through Shippensburg with the freighters. Some of it fell out into the pockets of John Cessna.

CHAPTER SEVENTEEN
The Glorious Years

John Cessna threw all of his weight behind the blow he leveled at Stephen's chin. The impact succeeded in throwing both of them to the ground.

John, Jr. was the younger and smaller of the two cousins, but this only made him try harder to get the upper hand.

Their fathers, John, and Stephen Cessna, could not help but laugh at themselves. History was replaying itself in the farmyard near Carlisle.

"You have to learn to duck once in a while, son," said Stephen, Sr. The boy rubbed his chin and contemplated what he had done wrong.

These were the glory years for the Cessna brothers. Crops and children flourished. Hunger and disease were quickly fading from their memory.

The men began to acquire land, and the women began to accumulate the trivial things which create the feeling of "civilization."

The Cessna brothers were now a comfortable twenty miles apart. This is just enough distance to allow them to cherish and love each other again.

They watched as their families grew into a community of mixed cultures. Germans, Quakers, Irish, and English (the new Americans) created a new heritage. The Cessna brothers were determined to bring the family closer together, and closer to their French roots.

On the first Sabbath of each month, weather permitting, the families joined for a two or three-day rendezvous. It was always held at Stephen's home. He was the oldest. The market at Carlisle was much more advantageous place for shopping.

John always brought items to sell at the market, and as he liked to say, "to pay for the trip."

The two families bonded together as the patriarchs told the stories of long ago France and the Irish exodus endured by their father. Their father's language was kept alive and passed to the new generation at those reunions.

The most solemn moment of each gathering came when Stephen retrieved the old Huguenot Bible from its hiding place, and read scripture in French.

The cousins all learned their place in the family dream. The teen boys tested each other with shooting skills, even though neither of the fathers was particularly fond of firearms.

Contests of running, horseback riding, and wrestling all developed spontaneously, as each cousin vied for status among the herd of children.

Remembering their father's lessons, John and Stephen guided the competition to greater focus on education. French and history lessons were added.

Team Shippensburg seemed to excel at the scholastics. John was the better teacher of the two brothers. Several of his children would become prominent community leaders because of the knowledge he imparted to them.

Another highlight of the family weekend was the ritual arm wrestling match between the two patriarchs. The children were greatly excited as these brothers squared off against each other, making a fine show of their competitive natures.

Stephen, the oldest and still the largest, usually dominated the event. But John could pull off a surprise every now and then. Their bond of love was strengthened with every test against each other.

Stephen's son John, his wife Pryscilla, and their children always made the short journey for the rendezvous as well. Though he lived in York County, he was less than 10 miles from Carlisle. This continued until John's premature death to a fever in 1751.

Pryscilla Foulke-Cessna was a Quaker girl. At John's death she would not relinquish her Quaker ties. She remarried a few years later and carried John's children to a new home in North Carolina.

Her children began to use the spelling "Sisney" once arriving in Guilford County.

The entire Cessna family was deeply shaken by the first death of a member in America. As the first born of his generation, John Cesna had carried the symbolic dreams of his namesake, the old French soldier.

His widow, however, rejected all pleas to move the children closer to the Cessna grandparents. Her father and Stephen Cessna had once had a bitter legal dispute. Stephen had her father's farm taken by the court and sold as a Sheriff's auction.

Pryscilla's children would never know the family traditions and history.

With the loss of Patience and her children to North Carolina, it became even more important to the Irish born brothers that their children understand they were not English or Irish. They may live under the rule of that King, but they were French!

Both Cessna men had a wealth of stories to tell the children about their father. Stephen held the family bible.

John Cessna had retained a token of his father's heritage as well: a silver Huguenot Cross, which their patriarch had often worn in battle. It became the family's precious icon.

The stories, their language, the Bible, and the silver cross became focal points of the family gatherings. And they became the heart of the family's identity.

CHAPTER EIGHTEEN
Foundation for War

The Irish and Scots were all Presbyterian of the "Blue Stocking" type. They were a hardy, brave, and hot-headed people: excitable in temper and un-restrainable in their passion. Their hand was as open to a friend as it was clenched against an enemy.

They loathed the Pope, all Catholics, and had little respect for the Quakers.

By moving these unruly people into Cumberland Valley, the Penn Family deliberately placed them in harm's way. They were set there to be a buffer.

They were positioned to take the brunt of any conflict with the natives. This comforted the peace loving Quakers.

It is an unfortunate coincidence that the natives being displaced by the influx of settlers were among the most vicious and vindictive of the tribes. The Delaware and Shawnee people were fermenting a deep hatred of the English newcomers.

In March of 1748, George Croghan took a large pack train of supplies through Shippensburg. He was on his way to his trading post at the Indian village of Logstown. An important Shawnee town, Logstown was about nineteen miles below the place where two great rivers became the mighty Ohio.

The Pennsylvania Council had sent him with £200 worth of goods. He was to use this to secure loyalty from the Western Tribes for future trading with the English. He was also hoping to discourage their relationships with the French.

In April, over 1500 warriors from various tribes showed up to receive the gifts (bribes). Croghan was overwhelmed and soon ran out of the government's gifts. To keep the crowd peaceful, he had to offer an additional £224 in powder, lead, knives, flints, brass wire, and tobacco from his own stock.

The warriors were appeased temporarily, but the meeting had two negative effects. The first was that it caused the French to double their efforts to win the loyalty of the Indians. The second was an uncontrollable, yet foreseeable side effect.

As teamsters returned from carrying all of those trade goods to Logstown, they passed through Shippensburg. It did not take long before everyone in the village had heard about the vast number of warriors just over Allegheny Mountain.

Both John Cessna Sr. and his brother Stephen heard and were alarmed by the report. Settlers began to arm themselves further. Militias increased their training. John Cessna increased the stock of arms he sold from his store.

What followed next only increased fear in the hearts of Shippensburg folks.

The Shawnee and Delaware again complained about squatters taking up land on the Juniata. In the Fall of 1753, Ben Franklin organized a large peace conference between the Pennsylvania Commissioners and as many Chiefs as they could invite.

The conference was held at the two-year-old town of Carlisle, just twenty miles from Shippensburg.

It was held less than 2 blocks from the house where Stephen and Patience Cessna lived.

Patience was so frightened by the crowd of natives that she refused to leave the house. She kept her doors barricaded. She felt a little better when her brother-in-law showed up carrying a rifle gun. He would be their house guest for the week of the conference.

John Cessna and other men from Shippensburg traveled quite frequently to the Cumberland County Seat. They had seen groups of warriors moving through the countryside around their town.

Now, these men were in Carlisle, watching as the crowd of natives kept growing larger and larger. The streets of Carlisle were filled with feather-crested Indian chiefs from the Ohio River, the far distant Miami River, and the lake country of the North.

John and Stephen sat up late at night discussing what they had seen that day. Neither man was convinced that Peace was going to come from these negotiations.

From her bed, Patience listened as the men discussed the danger which was lurking all around them.

The atmosphere was heavy with fear and terror. The settlers from the nearby farms came to see the spectacle and hear the news. Ben Franklin worried that with so many Europeans and Natives mixing in the town, that trouble might break out.

The Peace Commissioners failed to show up with any presents to give to the Chiefs and their warriors. For three very tense days there was a great deal of grumbling among both whites and natives. The visitors began stealing food when none was offered to them.

When told that gifts would arrive later, and asked if the peace talks could begin, one of the chiefs replied that his "people could and would not do any public business while the blood of their tribe remained upon their garments, and that nothing would wash it unless the presents intended to cover the graves of the departed were actually spread upon the ground before them."

Eventually the presents arrived, but an atmosphere of mistrust had already been established.

The vast number of warriors walking past their homes did little to assure the people of Shippensburg and Carlisle that peace was within reach.

Tensions remained high for the families in Shippensburg. The isolated farmers in Shippen's Farm started to make emergency plans...just in case.

John Cessna headed back to his home with the discouraging news.

Patience now began to beg Stephen to get a rifle for each of their sons. She was convinced that they needed it to protect themselves.

CHAPTER NINETEEN
The First Indian War

The troubles began in 1754.

The French decided to prevent English settlers from moving any further West than they already had. They established a line of forts from Presque Isle on Lake Erie down to Fort Duquesne (Pittsburgh) at the place where two rivers, with unpronounceable names, became the Ohio River.

France drew the proverbial line in the sand. They insisted that the English go no further, and dared them to try. The Delaware and Shawnee people were delighted to see this barrier to English migration. They wanted no English settlers West of the Blue Mountains.

Actually, the French only cared about the Fur Trading business. The English settlers were not so much of a problem for them. It was the traders wandering into present day Ohio, Kentucky and Indiana that threatened to harm their profits. The homesteaders, however, were the heart of the issue for the natives.

The governor of Virginia was not about to relinquish his door to the Golden West. Most of their traders traveled through the place of the three rivers. Now, they found Fort Duquesne blocking that place.

George Washington was sent with a small party to "invite" the French to vacate Fort Duquesne. Shooting erupted. Washington and the French blamed each other for starting the fight.

French Lieutenant Jumonville was captured by Washington, and mysteriously murdered while prisoner.

Slanderous accusations were then exchanged, resulting in a war between France and England which would involve battlefields in every hemisphere of the planet.

The Seven Years' War (1756–1763) is widely considered to be the first global conflict in human history. It was a struggle for world supremacy between Great Britain and France

At the most violent center of this conflict were the bitter Delaware and Shawnee people who had been displaced. They were pitted against the newly arrived Scots Irish settlers of Cumberland Valley.

After George Washington failed, England sent General Braddock to finally kick the French out of Fort Duquesne and the Ohio River county.

In the Spring of 1755 General Braddock began to gather a fully equipped army for the task before him.

In June, John and Stephen Cessna spent an entire monthly rendezvous discussing Braddock's Army. They knew this meant that war was on the horizon. This was the last monthly gathering of the Cessna family that was ever held.

Because the Quakers who controlled the Pennsylvania government would not invest any money or manpower on defense, each community began construction of its own fort or stockade.

Robert Chambers had founded Chambersburg, about twelve miles West of Shippensburg. He built a large, fortified stone house and stockade around a spring.

His community was much smaller than Shippensburg. But his fort was much stronger. It was the strongest fortification for seventy-five miles in any direction.

Chambers even installed lead sheets on the roof so fire arrows could not penetrate it. He managed to get two swivel cannon and a goodly number of muskets for defense.

In Shippensburg, the settlers organized themselves to construct Fort Franklin. It was little more than a stockade with a couple of storerooms.

John and Agnes Cessna were delighted that the new fort was less than five hundred feet from their home on King Street. The warrior's path between Cessna and Widow Piper's Tavern was now officially the central street of the village.

John Cessna joined other men at the Widow's Tavern for an unofficial town meeting. They suggested that the fort be built on two unleased lots belonging to their absentee landlord, Edward Shippen.

Others quickly joined by suggesting that they get materials for the fort by depleting the timber on Shippen's other properties in the area.

Shippen would pay for the stockade, but the people would have to build it themselves. Every man from the surrounding farms turned out on the day appointed to build the crude fortress.

Alexander Culbertson suggested that they name the place after the only politician who understood what danger they faced. Ben Franklin was already at work making plans for the safety of those settlers on the frontier,

Associated militias were formed and two of the men from Shippensburg were chosen as officers: Alexander Culbertson and James Dunlap. John Cessna was determined to keep his sons out of this war and prayed it might pass quickly.

But no one had ever seen this kind of war before.

Cessna was not the only Pennsylvanian hoping the war would pass them by. The Supreme Council insisted that this fight belonged to Virginia and General Braddock.

The Quaker mindset of the Supreme Council voted down every proposal that called for preparation for war. They insisted that there had to be peaceful ways to defuse the threatening conflict.

At the western end of the province, the French had no trouble convincing the Delaware and Shawnees to call the war dance. The forests around Fort Duquesne and the forks of the Ohio River filled with war parties.

General Braddock began to organize his army at Fort Cumberland, just one hundred miles southeast of Fort Duquesne. He made no effort to keep his intentions a secret.

Braddock intended to cut a military road through the wilderness, permanently linking the forks of the Ohio to the Potomac River and Virginia.

Ben Franklin loved to use the power of his printing house to shape public opinion. His pamphlet *Plain Truth* had resulted in the organization of the "Militia Associations."

In April of 1755, Franklin sent a new round of flyers throughout the counties of Lancaster, York, and Cumberland. In it, he argued that the settlers should help by providing wagons and horses for Braddock's army.

Franklin hinted that if teamsters did not offer themselves voluntarily, the provincial quartermaster might go with armed men and seize what animals and equipment was needed. If you wanted to be paid, you should volunteer.

In a few weeks, two hundred wagons and 250 pack horses, manned by men from the counties West of the Susquehanna (Cumberland and York), came through the valleys to meet Braddock at Fort Cumberland.

Stephen Cessna, Jr. and John Cessna, Jr. were among those who hired out for the baggage train.

The two Irish born brothers, were in great anguish as they watched their eldest sons go off to war.

The Cessna family were businessmen. The boys were merely excited about the profit to be made. They were sure that teamsters would be well paid, but have little fighting to do.

Braddock was overconfident. The French garrison at Fort Duquesne was fairly small. He had two times as many soldiers as did the French.

Though he received numerous warnings, Braddock was convinced that the Indians would be no match for the mightiest army in the world.

In addition to the regular soldiers, Braddock had several hundred militia men from Virginia and New Jersey. He now outnumbered the French garrison by four to one. Again, he failed to calculate how many Indians there might be.

Braddock bragged that it would be a short war. He was partly right. His part would be short.

The army started North, cutting, and building a road as it crawled through the wilderness. Every step was counted by the silent eyes of the natives who followed their progress. The forest was filled with spies.

As the entourage approached Fort Duquesne, the French forces came out to meet Braddock's troops. Both sides prepared to fight a European style battle in the midst of a forest.

But several thousand Indians who filled the woods around them, had no intention of fighting like that. On July 9th, the fighting started before either the French or English troops could assume proper formations.

The Indians assumed their usual type of warfare. Hiding behind rocks, trees, and brushes they would pop into view for a brief moment and fire a shot. They reloaded from hidden positions, and fired again.

The Virginia militia men who had come with Braddock immediately jumped into the forest and began to engage them in like manner. They were soon fighting hand to hand with an enemy who vastly outnumbered them. The Virginians began to die.

Braddock insisted that the regular army stand in the road and return fire in organized volleys. They fought the only way they had been trained to fight.

The officers shouted at the men to fire. But the men begged for targets.

The English soldiers could see nothing but puffs of gun smoke among the foliage. The Redcoats began to fall in piles along the path.

Ordered to make a bayonet charge on a low ridge, one company just refused. They could not see any enemy to fight.

The forest was filled with terrifying war screams. But the enemy remained invisible. The entire company, and its officers, died right there on the path.

Officers threatened to shoot any cowards who refused to stand in the open, or tried to take cover. When the Indians shot the officers from their horses, there was no one was left to give orders.

General Braddock was severely wounded as well. Those who were still alive began a panicked retreat. But the road was blocked by the enormous baggage train.

Utter chaos blocked the new road. Men were running for their lives. Teamsters dumped their baggage, cut horses loose from wagons, and rode bareback for home. Now the road, filled with hundred of piles of supplies and abandoned wagons blocked their escape.

When they saw the mass of men running for their lives away from the fighting, Stephen, Jr. and John, Jr. joined the frantic exodus. Neither ever saw the fighting. But they could hear the blood curdling war cries surrounding them and erratic firing of guns in the distance.

The Cessna cousins left most of their horses behind them. It was a disaster!

One thousand four hundred and sixty men went into the woods to make war. They were followed by several hundred women and camp followers.

Before the sun set on 9 July 1755, 456 soldiers were lying dead in the military road they had just built. Another 421 were wounded and crawled into the woods to hide from the savages. They died there, waiting for help which never came.

No one was able to count how many women and camp followers perished in the forest.

Braddock died of his wound on July 13th as he and the few survivors limped back to Fort Cumberland. He was buried in the middle of his road. Horses and wagons were run over the grave to erase any trace of it. This denied the Indians a chance to desecrate it.

Of his three Virginia companies, Col George Washington said, "they behaved like men and died like soldiers"; and that "scarce thirty men were left alive." One of those thirty men was Daniel Boone.

Washington was one of a very few officers who survived the battle without any wounds at all. Two horses had been shot from under him, and his coat had numerous bullet holes.

Of the eighty-nine officers in Braddock's command, sixty-three were killed or wounded beyond the ability to provide leadership. The might of the British military in America had been nearly eliminated.

Men began to retreat back into Cumberland Valley with tales of the horrific slaughter.

General Dunbar had been stationed at Fort Cumberland with a small army to serve as Braddock's reserve force. His post was overrun with desperate refugees from the fight, trickling down the road in an alarming fashion.

At all hours, for three days and nights, groups would come to the gate with loud wails of terror and tragedy.

"Braddock is dead." "The Army is wiped out!"

"There are 10,000 Indians right behind us."

General Dunbar wrote to Governor Morris and announced that he could not defend this post and was withdrawing his force to "Winter Quarter" in Philadelphia. It was Summer.

The frontier was now totally undefended. The valleys of Pennsylvania, Maryland, and Virginia were wide open and vulnerable.

The Delaware, Shawnee, and other tribes were drunk with their victory. Having captured all of the Army's whiskey and rum, many were indeed drunk.

It took two months for the Indians to complete their victory celebration. It took that long to be sure they had scavenged everything valuable from the thousand bodies scattered over the forest floor. Just retrieving the abandoned baggage and catching the loose livestock took weeks.

By mid-September, the Indians were ready to resume the war. They were now the best equipped army on the continent, having retrieved over one thousand rifles, countless barrels of powder, and hundreds of pounds of lead.

The warriors broke up into parties of 50 to 100 braves. They headed East to drive every English settler back over the Susquehanna River.

This was no longer just a war between the French and the English. The natives were releasing decades of frustration and hatred for people living on their land.

This war did not come marching down the roadways in a colorful parade as the Europeans were used to. This war came wafting over the mountain passes like a deadly fog. The warriors brought death when and where it was least expected.

The first attack came at Penn's Creek, above Harris' Ferry. The community of twenty-six peaceful Germans, disappeared in an hour's time.

One wounded man was able to escape and carry word to Harris' Ferry. The men who rushed to the rescue found the mutilated bodies of thirteen old men and children, including a two-week-old baby. The rest had been carried into captivity.

The settlers had been watching for attacks coming from the West. But the Indians, knowing they would be carrying booty and captives on the return trip, simply slipped around the settlements. When they had made it as far as the Susquehanna River, they turned and headed West again, killing as they came. Having marked the easier targets on their way East, they now left a path of horror and destruction behind as they traveled back to their homes.

Chambersburg, Shippensburg, and Carlisle had appeared to be too formidable for an easy conquest, so they were bypassed. The surrounding farms and isolated travelers did not do so well.

On 13 November 1755, the *Pennsylvania Gazette* printed a long (but partial) list of those persons who had been killed or taken captive in the coves of Cumberland County. Horrors of the Indian's rage were reported up and down the frontier.

The "Widow Piper's" had become the headquarters for the Public Safety Committee of Shippensburg. Each morning men would gather to share news and give advice about how to keep your family safe.

The best advice seemed to be "Pack up and go back East."

John Cessna heard two stories which made his heart cold with fear.

The first was told by the first generation of this family born in America.

John, Jr. and Stephen, Jr. had returned from Braddock's defeat with stories about how disorganized and "ignorant" the British army was. They described how Braddock had managed to recruit about sixty of the Indians from southern Virginia to serve as scouts.

Had he listened to them, the massacre would have been avoided.

Instead, considering them of no value, Braddock had ignored them. Indian scouts were kept out of strategy talks and left to wander around the camp.

Many braves had brought their families with them. The squaws soon learned that there was potential for wealth by flirting and cavorting with the crimson-robed soldiers.

Stephen, Jr. pronounced with disgust that the officers' fondness for the Indian maids was "scandalous."

Chief White Thunder had brought his daughter. The girl lived up to her name of "Bright Lightning," and caused many a competitive scuffle among the soldiers.

Eventually, the braves got jealous of the white's attention to their women. The entire group deserted.

The end result was Braddock had been completely without the help of any Indian scouts.

In early October, Thomas Fossit returned to his home in Shippensburg. He told in great detail about the battle and claimed that he had shot General Braddock himself.

"The Gen'rl insisted that everyone stand up like brave soldiers and fight. But there wasn't anybody to fight like that. Them injuns was all hiding in the trees. Them soldiers died standing in the lane, just like turkeys," Fossit lamented.

"Me and my brother Joseph was just supposed to be driving the ammunition wagons. We was ducked down behind the bushes when the General rides up a cussing and screaming. 'Stand up and fight brave!' he shouts, 'I'll kill any coward.'

"The Gen'l focused on my brother and starts yelling at him to stand up. When Joseph finally said 'NO,' the General called him a coward and shot him down with a pistol.

"I couldn't believe it," Fossit continued. "Quick as I could reload, I put a bullet in the General's side. I am sure it was my shot that killed the man." All his life, Fossit would brag that he had killed the General for being such an idiot and killing his own men.

In his latter years, Fossit operated a tavern near the place where Braddock was buried. He shared his story as gospel to anyone who would listen. He did so until he was an old man.

Fossit made it his life's goal to let everyone know what a madman their "Glorious General Braddock" really was.

The terror of war with the Indians was about to become everyday life for the next three decades. From October 1755 until the deep snows of 1756, the attacks continued. Death settled in on the valleys of Pennsylvania. An estimated 1,200 people were slaughtered or carried into captivity that winter.

People moved from their farms into the villages. Soon, there were four and five families living to a house in both Shippensburg and Carlisle. Some families kept running until they were back in their former homes, East of the Susquehanna River.

John Cessna's tavern was filled with refugees. It was also filled with horses and teamsters. Because of the fighting, many of the trade caravans were stopped at Shippensburg. They were afraid to go any further without an armed escort. They could not go on, and felt that they could not go back either.

CHAPTER TWENTY
The summer of 1756

By the following March, the people of Western Pennsylvania were huddled together in crowded cabins throughout the valleys and coves. Remote settlers had moved to the villages, and the towns were overcrowded with refugees.

No government relief was in sight, and the compassion of their neighbors was their only help.

Travel was unthinkable. The Indians seemed to be everywhere! When the snow melted from the passes, everyone knew that even more war parties would be coming among their homes.

In 1756, the situation was even worse than they imagined. The numbers of war parties would be double what it had been in 1755.

Every man and every gun represented a valuable asset to protect the community. It was considered unpatriotic for a man to visit the next town unless he had permission of the local Committee of Public Safety. By absenting yourself, you would be leaving your friends weaker in their defenses.

Every supply train had to be protected by armed parties.

Family conversations took a dire turn. Instead of "the Injuns might get you," parents now warned "**when** the Indians come ...."

Being attacked seemed inevitable to the terrified people. They began to look for ways to survive the attack.

"When they come, you should hide in here!" parents began to tell their children.

"When they come, you must run as fast as you can."

Survivors who escaped from captivity, told stories which were repeated at every hearth. The homesteaders gradually gained an understanding of the type of war this would be.

It was seldom that the savages killed everyone they came upon. Usually the slaughter would stop the moment people surrendered.

Those taken captive had a chance of surviving. The bounty paid by the French was higher for prisoners than for scalps. But only the fittest could survive the prisoner's journey.

A few people had escaped and returned to tell them what was happening. Young people were admonished that those who surrendered had a better chance for survival.

The Cessna clan no longer held its monthly meeting. The two halves of the family were separated by twenty miles of what had become a killing zone.

It became necessary for John Cessna's family to spend most of their time in town. He owned three outlying farms by 1756. Now, all labor on those farms was done at significant risk.

All of the Cessna men began to keep horses and guns at the ready. They needed to fight, and to respond to any cries for help.

On April 6th of 1756 John Cessna, Sr. and his neighbors were gathered once again at Widow Piper's. Alexander Culbertson rode up to where the men sat. His urgency was obvious.

Just as obvious was the fact that this was Captain Culbertson of the militia, not just their friend, Alex.

In rushed phrases he explained that Shingas, a well-known Delaware war chief, and a large party of warriors had attacked and destroyed Fort McCord. This was a family fort less than twenty miles from Shippensburg. The Indians had killed or captured all twenty-seven of the settlers there. Three companies of the militia were being called up to give chase.

Captain Culbertson was here to mobilize his company. Without hesitation, every man at the tavern grabbed a rifle and headed for his horse.

Of the three companies to give chase after the Indians, only Culbertson's from Shippensburg was mounted. Horses were a ready commodity in this hub of transportation.

John Cessna, who had never been in combat before and barely knew how to use his musket, was now riding to war with forty-nine of his neighbors pressed closely around. John, Jr. was riding with younger men in the rear. Everyone's stomach churned in fear.

The truth is that John Cessna should have stayed home that day. He was 57 years old, yet still fit. He honestly did not know how to fight. But he had no intention of not doing his duty.

Because they were mounted, Culbertson's Company covered more ground than the other companies. Not knowing which pass Shingas might take, they had ridden directly North and then followed Blue Mountain its entire swing to the South. On the third day, they found the tracks of the war party and realized they were not far behind the Indians.

Benjamin Blythe, Cessna's next door neighbor, announced "They are headed for Sideling Hill Creek! I know how we can cut them off."

He bolted through the underbrush on his horse. The rest of the troop followed.

It was a mad rush through the forest. Desperation filled every heart.

John had no idea where he was or where he was going. He just followed the rump of the horse in front of him. After a hot, sweaty, and thirsty hour, they came upon the creek just as Blythe had predicted.

The company raced along the East bank.

On the other side John could catch glimpses of Indians racing in the same direction. It seemed obvious that both parties were headed towards a place up ahead of them.

It was indeed a race to get to a place of advantage. Every settler, every Indian, and every one of their captives knew a fight was moments away.

A creek or river was a serious obstacle to fighting this kind of warfare. Crossing it puts you in the open for 20 to 40 yards. You became an easy target.

If the stream was crossed without care, you might foul your weapon or ammunition with the splashing.

There was a shallow ford ahead which Blythe and Captain Culbertson had chosen for the confrontation.

Shingas was aware of it also, and was pushing his warriors towards the spot. He knew he had to get his people across it before the whites could set up an ambush.

The first shot came as a great shock to John Cessna. He dismounted and looked for a tree to hide behind. His horse immediately ran off into the forest.

Once settled, he tried to identify the locations of his friends. He could only see half a dozen of his fellow militia. He had no idea where his son might be.

Then John, Sr. looked across the creek for the enemy. They seemed to be everywhere, but seldom were visible long enough for him to take a shot.

The confusion was crushing. The thick smoke of the black powder hung low over the forest floor and soon created a bluish fog.

The war cries of the savages were piercing. But they were not as frightening as the screams of men being struck by musket balls.

The fighting was fierce for over two hours. John was trying to load and fire as fast as he could. He was never sure if he was doing the right thing or not. And he was suddenly aware that he had not brought enough ammunition.

The Indians kept moving from tree to tree, hoping to get the settlers to use up their ammunition. Without their guns, the fighting would become hand to hand, and the natives had a clear advantage.

The warriors were also seeking to get an angle of vantage on the white men hiding behind trees.

John Cessna could never tell if he hit any of the enemy with his shooting. The tree protecting him held many scars of bullets and arrows, but he was unscathed.

His confusion and self-doubt were crippling. With no clear battle lines, and no one to give him directions, he felt completely alone.

The business of death was being conducted all around him. He had never been more frightened.

For one brief moment, John worried that the old French soldier would be ashamed of his performance in battle.

He had no way of knowing that his father's confusion and terror at the Battle of Boyne were remarkably similar to what he was experiencing that day along Sideling Hill Creek.

Like his father, he held his place and continued fighting with the raw courage in his heart. He could not bring himself to run away when his neighbors were fighting and dying all around him.

He prayed that the younger John Cessna was still safe.

Suddenly, John heard new firing in the distance. Captain Chambers and the company from Chambersburg had been on foot. Hearing the shooting, they came running and approached the battle from the Indian's rear. They were on the opposite side of the creek from Culbertson's company.

The Chambersburg men engaged in hand-to-hand combat before they could get any battle lines drawn. Though valiant, they were unprepared for the fight they had found.

Many of Chamber's men died in the first few minutes of arriving at the battle.

The savages began to slip away to the North, and the militia had neither the strength nor the ammunition to pursue them.

John Cessna and his friends began to survey the battle. It was a heavy loss.

Captain Alexander Culbertson had been killed. Also killed were Francis Scott who owned a store, William Boyd, Jacob Payntor, and John Reynolds. Reynolds was the neighbor just east of Shippensburg, and a close friend.

Twenty men from Captain Chambers' company of thirty, were lying dead along the hillside.

But it was the wounded that disturbed John the most. Benjamin Blythe, his neighbor to the West, was gravely wounded in the chest. Francis Campbell, his neighbor in town, had a bullet clean through his thigh and was bleeding badly. A half-dozen other men from Shippensburg looked as though they might die if they did not get help soon.

The dead were quickly buried along the creek, and the Battle of Sideling Hill would go down in history as the colonist's warning that they were not yet ready for this kind of war. Their failure was a shock to each of them.

Using the few horses which hadn't run off, they carried the wounded back to Shippensburg. John Cessna, Jr. made a heroic ride. He raced the 20-plus miles to Shippensburg and gave a report. Grabbing another horse, he raced twenty miles further to Carlisle to bring back the only surgeon in the valley. Shippensburg's only doctor was among those missing after the fighting.

Both Surgeon and messenger were back in town waiting when the bloody survivors arrived.

Of the fifty men who rode with Captain Culbertson that day, 40 (80%) were killed, wounded, or missing. The company of militia which was supposed to protect Shippensburg no longer existed.

In Carlisle...Stephen Cessna had gathered his family close.

Word had come to them that Pryscilla, the wife of John, had remarried. Her new husband, Abraham Elliott, had inherited John's property, sold it, and taken Stephen's grandchildren to start a new life in Guilford County, North Carolina. The loss had broken the old man's heart, but at least the children were far from the fighting.

Stephen, Jr., Theo, and Thea shared the house on town lot #187. Stephen and Patience had purchased it two years earlier. Their son Thomas, his wife Margaret, and infant Stephen spent much their time with them as well.

Thomas insisted on returning to his farm three times each week to tend to the most urgent matters. But the family stayed close in town.

In might seem strange, but the war had brought a good deal of prosperity to the community. At least the tavern and shopkeepers were doing well.

People struggled to continue a normal life. They just had to avoid traveling outside of town.

With so many people crowded into town, there was time to shop and discover what bright things were available.

It was on dreary day in late March of 1756 when Stephen and his daughter went window shopping through Carlisle. Thea stopped her father in front of Daniel Hogan's hat shop and decided to practice her 15-year-old girlish charm.

"Pa, don't you need a new hat? Your old one is so ... so OLD!"

In truth, Stephen had no inadequate feelings about his hat at all. It was perfectly functional and fit him well. Now, his daughter's criticism made him question it. She was pretty smart about fashion and looking good. Maybe she was right.

"Let's just take a look," she prodded. "It can't hurt to look!" and she pushed her father into the shop.

"Pa needs a new hat," she announced to the proprietor.

Then as quick as a mouse she spun to the left and flashed a smile at young Daniel Hogan who was sitting in the corner. At 17 years of age, young Daniel was still a bit awkward, but showing a little potential to the young ladies of the town.

The senior Daniel began to make a sales pitch to Stephen. Pushing his best hats into the old man's hands one at a time, he began singing their praises. A hat was an important part of a man's wardrobe.

The young people took advantage of the adult's distraction to begin a shy dance of "noticing" each other. Thea giggled nervously.

"What do you think of this one?" Stephen eventually asked his daughter. She spun away from young Daniel so fast that her skirt blossomed. The boy took notice.

"Oh no, Pa!" she lamented.

Stephen wondered why she had flashed a quick smile at the gangly-looking lad in the corner. He looked to be a worthless lout.

"You need something more special. That hat is too ordinary. In fact, all these hats are too ordinary!"

Thea had a way of commanding any situation. Her strawberry hair and green eyes had a magical power on the males of the species. And their age did not seem to diminish the effect she had on them either.

Thea started a long discourse of her opinions on such matters as dignified hats.

In a short while, she had her father and both of the Hogan men convinced. Stephen Cessna was ready for the most distinctive headwear in the village. He needed something so dignified that no other man in the county would have anything similar.

Stephen needed a white hat, she announced with such conviction that the men did not dare disagree.

No one else in town had such a thing. It would set him apart in a worthy manner. The shopkeeper admitted he could make such a thing, but it would take time.

He had to bleach the horsehair, pound it into felt, then it needed to be cut and sewn to fit. It might take a week or more. Perhaps he could find a hunter with a white pelt that could be used to make the felt, he pondered aloud.

In the end, Thea decided for him, it would be made of bleached wool. The lanolin in the wool would make it waterproof.

His daughter's charm had Stephen convinced. She was quite proud of herself. He did not even protest at the higher than usual price. It was a sure sign that he was fully under his daughter's spell.

As they left the shop she grabbed his elbow and snuggled close to him. This brought the smile for which she had hoped.

The young woman strolled home victorious. Her father was under her charm. And young Daniel Hogan was beginning to notice her as well. Everything seemed right in the world for Thea Cessna.

The stories of Indian atrocities continued with such regularity that they became a routine backdrop. People continued to live as normal as possible, they just had to plan any trip outside of the town.

Instead of a solitary daily chore, farming was now something done in groups, with everyone carrying a fire lock gun.

It took two weeks for Daniel Hogan to create "the hat." He was quite proud of himself and planned to repeat the process for a new line of products. He put his best effort into making a sterling hat for Mr. Cessna.

It would be the only one in town, but only for a short while. He planned to make it so perfect that others would come seeking one for themselves. This was going to be good for business.

On the day he finished it, he was so excited that he could not wait for the customer to wander back in. If he had young Daniel deliver it today, he reasoned, he could start hearing the compliments that much quicker.

So the boy was dispatched with the gleaming white hat.

In his own excitement, Hogan did not read the boy's enthusiasm for another encounter with the green-eyed, red-haired girl.

Patience told the boy that Stephen and the others were about a mile outside town at Thomas' farm. They would be back towards dark, she told him.

"Yes," she said, "Thea is with them. But it isn't safe for you to go out there."

The boy explained that his father would not approve of him leaving the hat anywhere but in

Stephen's own hands. In his mind he reasoned that if he took it directly to the farm, he might get to visit with Thea.

The run to the farm had been easy enough, but left the boy breathless. A look into those green eyes made him forget any exhaustion.

The men were in awe by the trophy he had brought. They began an instant discussion about its virtues and quality.

The two young people smiled widely at each other as the men gave due admiration to the new hat. Forgotten for a moment, the two young people slipped away from the others.

"Come with me," Thea enticed. And he went.

They ran behind the barn. Daniel expected they would stop there. But the redhead ran into the woods. When he hesitated, she grabbed his hand and pulled him along.

"It's not far."

Scarcely thirty yards into the woods she halted by a small spring. Daffodils were making their annual appearance and the place was beautiful. He was taking it all in when she grabbed his shoulders, pulled him down and kissed him.

It was the first kiss for both of them. It was designed to bring him fully under her spell. It worked completely.

But fate had other plans for them.

As young Daniel stared in disbelief, a long shaft with a white crystal point emerged from Thea's throat and blood began to run down the front of her dress. She had a look of shock on her face. She tried to speak but was unable to make any sound.

In an instant, three warriors leapt into the clearing. One struck the girl with a club, knocking her to the ground. His next move was to cut a circle of her red hair from the crown of her head in two quick sweeping motions.

Knowing that some English wore gold or silver crosses around their neck, the savage tore the girl's dress open to check.

A second of the warriors stood over young Daniel with his club raised. Immediately the boy surrendered. He was their captive.

Pushing him ahead of them, they led the terrified lad into the dense forest. Daniel Hogan was never seen or heard of again. He simply vanished.

Barely ten minutes had passed when the men noticed that the young people had disappeared. A call for them yielded no answer.

The men grabbed their guns and began an immediate search. It did not take long to find the girl's body.

Stephen was devastated at the sight.

"Indians! They must have known we were close and killed her to keep her from crying out," Stephen, Jr. said in a faint voice.

He did not mention that the white crystal arrowhead was a trademark of Captain Jack, a feared Shawnee Chief.

John and Thomas ran a short way through the woods looking for the missing boy, but gave up quickly. They were afraid that they might be outnumbered.

Theophilus carried his twin sister back to the wagon.

Stephen was lost in the horrible visage of his precious daughter. The dearest place in his heart had been dealt a crushing blow.

He kept remembering her torn dress and wondered if the Hogan boy had done that. He began to focus his anger over this loss on the silly boy who had put his daughter in harm's way.

"Damn that lad," he kept muttering to himself.

The group headed home, leading their dazed father behind a wagon which carried a bitter cargo.

Daniel Hogan was told. He and a group of men ran back to the farm and gave search.

Neighbor women came to prepare Thea's body, and a gloomy crowd gathered at the Cessna home.

At some point in the long evening, Stephen rose from his fog and entered the room where the girl's body lay in repose. Someone had brought the white hat and it lay near his precious daughter.

Its brightness caused him pain. Cursing it, he flung it into the fire and it was caught in a bright blaze.

His anger burned brighter than the hat.

Towards midnight the posse returned empty-handed. Daniel Hogan stopped in front of the house and Stephen Cessna lost all control of himself.

"Where is my daughter?" he screamed. "Give me my daughter back!"

Both men were drenched in angry tears.

Doubly shaken, Hogan backed away.

"Where is my son?" he quietly said to himself over and over again.

Somehow, the grief of these two men became focused on each other, and on "the hat."

Barely five days later, the two grieving fathers met by chance at an inn where Cessna was numbing his pain with whiskey.

"Where is my daughter?" he screamed at his former friend.

Flustered, Hogan responded with, "Where's the money for my hat?"

"You will never get a penny of my money for that worthless hat," babbled Cessna.

He stumbled towards the other man and struck a blow. It carried all of his bitterness and pain. In seconds, both men were in a bloody tangle on the floor, and their friends were separating them.

The hat became the symbol of blame for the day. It had just been two innocent young children, flirting in the Spring air. But now it became an admission of guilt.

For if Cessna were to pay, it felt like he would be admitting his daughter's death was somehow his fault. This was unthinkable.

For Hogan to relent and not collect for the hat would be admitting that he was at fault for the tragedy. This was equally unthinkable.

They began a public argument, seeking to recruit others to side with their point of view. Their passion grew as the debate grew.

Daniel Hogan thought to use the courts to get Cessna to relent. Pennsylvania still held the medieval debtor laws of England. He could have the old man put in jail until he paid. So he did just that.

At the April 1756 session of the Cumberland County Court, Stephen Cessna reported that he was in jail for an unjust debt of a hat, at the suit of Daniel Hogan.

The jail was a stone hut on East the side of the town square. It held no amenities, nor comforts of any kind. Only bars protected the door and window.

Stephen Cessna, Sr. could have been released at any time if he had paid for the hat. But his heart would not allow him. Moreover, as long as he stayed in jail, his protagonist was accountable to pay the expenses for keeping him there.

Two wounded hearts became locked in stalemate and a notorious feud. Neither would give, yet neither felt they would find peace in their hearts until the other gave in.

The tragedy was that Stephen Cessna and Daniel Hogan were both stubborn men. And their determination was fueled by the fierce pain of the loss of two beautiful children.

Stephen Cessna stayed in that jail for two years. He refused to relent, even when he was sick with fever and dysentery.

His wife hired a lawyer to intercede for him at the October 1757 court session, But both he and Hogan still refused any compromise. The petition describes him as "sick and in jail."

Stephen Cessna died in that frigid stone cell during the Winter of 1757-58. No one, and nothing, could dissuade him from his anger-driven stance.

Still unrelenting, Daniel Hogan pursued his losses in the court and caused the Cessna property to be seized by the Sheriff. The sheriff sold it at public auction on the 17th of April 1758.

Hogan finally had the last word on the issue. He finally got paid for the hat.

But through it all, he lost every friend he had in the town, and never found any satisfaction. In the end, two lives destroyed themselves in grief over the loss of two innocent lives.

On May 13 of 1756, the most notorious family feud in Cumberland County history was just getting started. Rev. Steel stepped into the pulpit of the little church at Silver Spring, three miles East of Carlisle.

He intended to preach about the sin of "unforgiveness," using these two men as his lesson.

Shortly after he started, a small man slipped in the back and whispered into the ear of the person on the aisle. One by one, the whisper spread through the congregation.

Finally, Rev. Steel understood that the newcomer had brought news of another attack. The family of William Walker had been wiped out and the marauders were headed towards Carlisle.

Offering a quick prayer to end the service and ask God for the ability shoot straight, the frontier minister dismissed the congregation.

"All who have a mind to, follow me," he announced.

Grabbing his hat and gun he raced from the church in hot pursuit. He was followed by a dozen men.

This became normal for the people of Western Pennsylvania. They struggled to maintain routine life. But they were ready in an instant to become militia, chasing down the marauders.

On September 1st, a group of such men gathered around the jail to bring Stephen Cessna further sad news. They had just returned from a three-day chase of a Shawnee war party.

His son, Stephen, Jr. had been killed in a posse similar to the one led by Rev. Steele that Sunday morning. The group had caught up with the raiding party and killed four of their number. But his son had not returned.

Another piece of Stephen's heart lay in the sylvan woodlands.

The two Cessna brothers, who were born in Ireland, seldom saw each other in that bloody year of 1756. It was a year of loss and grief. It was estimated that another 1,500 persons perished or disappeared at the hands of the red man that year.

The death toll continued to mount throughout the year. The Indians grew bolder. They even attacked funeral parties when the settlers sought to bury their dead in the countryside.

Government officials worked feverishly to negotiate for peace. But the powers inciting the war were far away in London and Paris.

CHAPTER TWENTY-ONE
Summer of 1757

In 1757 the war parties returned in even larger numbers. This year, the French had recruited tribes from Michigan, Canada, and Ohio to join in the killing.

The settlers were becoming more adept at protecting themselves. Terroristic wars are always a dance of surprise, adapt, surprise, and adapt again.

The government was sending more arms and troops into the frontier. Family stockades were replaced with professional forts.

The rifle gun, invented by Swiss and German gunsmiths in Lancaster, was becoming ever more available. It gave a distinct advantage of distance to the settlers. It was able to kill an Indian at six hundred feet instead of the 50 to 100 provided by unrifled muskets.

"Mère de Dieu! Quel scoundrell. Quel voleur! The man is a thief and a scoundrel!"

Agnes Cessna had never seen her husband in such a rage. He stormed through the large room of their cabin, throwing his hat at the wall.

It was mid-July of 1757.

"If Edward Shippen thinks I am going to take this lying down, he has another 'think' coming to him. He and his partner, George Croghan, swore that the Indians were pacified and happy. Now look at what is happening to the countryside. Shippen only cares about making his fortune and to hell with us settlers."

Shippensburg was crowded with refugees from Raystown (Bedford) and isolated farms to the West. John Cessna, a good business-minded person, had actually been making considerable cash off of these transients.

These people fled with little of the comforts of life, and even less to eat. So they were eager to trade cash and possessions for those necessities.

Croghan and Sir William Johnson had been able to keep the Iroquois tribes in New York allied with the

English settlers, but not the Shawnee, Delaware, Ottawa, and Miami tribes. These were heavily influenced by the French Commander at Detroit.

The French provided guns, powder, shot, and blankets for any war party that would strike out for the settlements of Pennsylvania, Virginia, and New York. When the parties returned, they were rewarded with cash or trade goods for every English scalp or captive they brought.

After today, Cessna vowed he would never again trust any Englishman.

The commander at Fort Franklin had ordered that all able-bodied men form a militia. He announced that taking turns, the militia would then follow each farmer to his fields and provide protection as they harvested.

Summer crops of wheat, barley and oats needed to be brought in. It was a particularly scorching summer and the crops were withering in the fields quicker than usual.

John had agreed that his three oldest boys (John, Jr., Charles, and Evan) should join the armed party. He had even donated a good amount of supplies the militia would need. Now he was handed his reward for being a loyal supporter of the community.

His farm would be among the LAST ones harvested!

He was beside himself in anger. He felt that Shippensburg owed him a better deal than this. The Cessnas had become an important part of this little settlement.

The militia commander thought that Cessna had already benefited quite handsomely from the situation, by selling victuals and supplies to the refugees.

In truth, John Cessna could have afforded the risk more than any of the other farmers. John was backed into a corner.

He had no adults left on the farm to help him. He had four sons and three daughters yet at home, but the oldest, Joseph, was in his 10th summer.

Cussing and discussing the situation in his father's tongue, John became quite a spectacle moving through the community. He even accused his neighbors of having bribed their preferred spot in the order of harvest.

Slowly he hatched a plan.

Approaching the two men who were next to last in line, Dennis O'Neidon and John Kirkpatrick, Cessna fanned the flames of their fear and bitterness.

"Shippen knows that our fields are the closest to being ready for harvest. He knows that if this heat keeps up, our wheat will 'shatter' before we can get to it. He hopes we will go broke this year, so we will have to borrow money from him or sell our places back to him.

"I'm telling you; the English are as crooked as snakes. Le mensonge d'un politicien a c'est propre spécial puent. I can smell their lies a mile off. We French and Irish have to stick together or they will destroy us. Je ne serai pas trompé! They aren't gonna cheat me!"

John proposed that the three men, accompanied by three boys, would strike out to harvest their own fields.

If the hot weather dried the crop anymore, the kernels would fall off the wheat stocks and be lost before they could be harvested. Every farmer knew you had to watch grain very closely at this time of year. It had to be cut before it could "shatter."

Cessna argued that since he was putting up all three muskets they would be taking, and that two of the boys would be his, his field should be worked first. Then they would work Kirkpatrick's field. At first light, Joseph, and Jonathan (age 10 & 8) followed their father to a place where they met Kirkpatrick and O'Neidon. Their friend, Joseph Kirkpatrick, also ten, was at his father's side. Cautiously they worked their way through the early morning haze to a field about one mile East of Shippensburg.

The sun grew hot as the morning progressed. The men continued to cuss their situation as they toiled (John in French and the others in Gaelic), guns close to hand.

The boys joked with each other and made a game of out of stacking the sheaves in positions that looked like imaginary people. A particularly fat one could pass for that parson who had come through the area last month. That made them all laugh, and Jonathan fell down holding his belly.

They were oblivious to the circumstances guiding their lives on this day.

At that moment, their boyhood ended.

At least six shots rang out from the surrounding forest. All three men went down and the boys were left frozen in place, their mouths open.

O'Neidon had been shot through the chest and died instantly. Kirkpatrick had been shot through the throat. Joseph watched as his father gasped for air and mouthed the word "RUN."

Cessna had been grazed across the back of his head and knocked to the ground. Only slightly dazed, he quickly rose.

As the boys watched in shock, nine warriors rushed from the woods. They had come down the trail over South Mountain, and stumbled on these men absorbed in their harvest.

The assailants streaked towards them through the wheat with their tomahawks raised high. None of the boys had presence of mind to flee. They stood like statues watching their fate unfold, as though in a slow motion dream.

"Attendez! Nous sommes le français!" screamed John Cessna, holding the back of his head in one hand, and holding the other hand, palm out, high above his head.

"Nous sommes le français! (We are French!)"

The first Indian to arrive at Joseph came to an abrupt halt and raised his tomahawk in the air.

"Français?"

"Oui, oui," cried John, looking at the boys.

"Oui, oui," feebly echoed Joseph and his brother.

The Indians look confused, but halted from their slaughter. In moments, the war party had gathered up the guns and powder. They also found the food that the party had brought with them.

Two of the savages scalped Kirkpatrick and O'Neidon. At this last act, Joseph Kirkpatrick got violently ill and began to throw up.

After a quick parley, one Indian stepped forward and commanded, "Venir! Come!" and started back into the woods.

John and the three boys reluctantly followed his lead. The other warriors followed on their heels.

Four hours later they had climbed to the top of Tuscarora Mountain. One of the savages ran forward and knocked John to the ground. They were tying his hands when the boys were pushed along the path, leaving their father.

The party was splitting.

One group was taking John and heading north towards New York. The remaining party pushed the three boys further West.

John was convinced he would never see his sons again. In his late fifties, he now faced the greatest physical challenge of his life.

His mind raced in search of options. Any hesitation on his part drew immediate physical abuse, and he knew he had no choice but to obey all commands instantly.

He knew that his captors were confused by his use of French. He kept playing their uncertainty for some kind of advantage.

That night, his feet were tightly bound and his hands bound behind him. Though it seemed impossible, sleep finally found him in the early hours before dawn.

He awoke to find himself alone in the forest.

He immediately began to struggle to free himself. *Now may be my only chance*, he thought desperately to himself. He pulled against the bindings so hard that his wrists began to bleed.

He was still doing so when the warriors returned and rewarded him with a heavy blow to his forehead and face. Now his nose was also bleeding.

Soon he looked like a frightful mess. He realized that his captors had been on another raiding party. Their arms were loaded with things stolen from someone's cabin.

With them was a girl of about 12 or 13. She was disheveled and crying hysterically.

Her hair was a brilliant blonde color, and it seemed she could only speak German. She gave a terrified shriek when she looked at John's bloody face.

John counted no less than five fresh scalps of the same blonde color. He assumed that the girl was the last living member of her family.

In the space of a few minutes, they were moving again. John and the girl were each given loads which seemed too great for them to carry. Each had a thong tied around their neck to make a choke leash of about ten feet in length. With it, they were pulled down the trail behind the braves.

The warriors only carried weapons and scalps. The two new slaves carried everything else.

For days, the party pushed through the rugged undergrowth of the dense forest. Eventually, they felt safe enough to return to main trails and began to make quicker travel towards the North.

John worked their confusion at every opportunity.

Two of the group were genuinely concerned that John was somehow one of their French allies and not the English enemy. They were convinced that they might be punished and not rewarded on their return.

Another offered that they might receive a handsome reward if they could get him to Presque Isle and the French officers there. So they moved ever North.

Somewhere in the midst of New York's wilderness, the part met a group of Iroquois and made a bargain to unload the worrisome burden that John had become. He had successfully talked his way out of the fate awaiting him.

The deciding factor that truly saved John Cessna was the chance encounter with a party of Seneca. He had been prisoner of a Wenro war party. Their territory was in the far West of New York.

The French soldiers at Fort Presque Isle (later to become Erie, PA) had enticed them to take the war path. Wenro were relatives of the Seneca, and both were part of the Iroquois League of six nations.

The Seneca immediately began to scold their cousins and remind them that they were allies of the English and that their behavior was "careless."

Allies of the English! John might be able to convince his new companions to carry him to British garrisons further East. He could not talk them into relinquishing the girl.

Being German, the Iroquois did not consider her an ally. Her desperate wailing as they led him away would haunt him forever.

It took the rest of the year, walking over five hundred miles, but John was able to make his way back to Shippensburg by Christmas. He was hardly the same man.

CHAPTER TWENTY-TWO
The Long Walk Home

At first John was treated as a prisoner. He remained bound until the Seneca returned him to their village and the elders could decide his fate. A lengthy conference, to which he was not invited, determined that he was a guest, not a prisoner.

He was finally freed. But not welcomed.

He was not a prisoner of war. He was not a slave. He was not a visiting dignitary. He had no real status in the village. And not being much of a curiosity, he was ignored.

He was told that eventually a party would go to the East and he could accompany them. Until then he would be fed. He was not given any comforts.

John had never been so poor, or so alone. He had never been without some kind of status or respect from those around him. It stripped him of all that he thought important about himself.

The long walk home was transformative to every part of his mind and body.

In about a week, a group took him with them to a village of the Cayuga. Another conference was held to decide if he was a prisoner or a guest. Eventually, warriors carried him to a Tuscarora town, and the process was repeated.

The Tuscarawas passed him to the Oneida, who in turn passed him to a Mohawk clan. On a day in late October, the Mohawk delivered him to Johnson Hall.

John was stunned at the outpost Sir William Johnson had built for himself. It was a glorious English manor at the edge of the wilderness. Johnson was the

King's official agent to the Iroquois. This placed him as a "middleman" in the lucrative trade for furs.

Johnson's wealth was overwhelming. An English-style estate of 400,000 acres, complete with large castle like house, was the foundation of what would become Johnstown, NY. It was like a mirage existing in the midst of the wilderness.

Indians of a least a dozen different tribes were camped in a random fashion around the large house. Business and trading were a daily activity. And business was brisk.

John Cessna's delivery to Johnson was without ceremony. The escorts told one of Johnson's men that they were returning a prisoner who had been taken by the French. They were given a package of trade goods in reward, and they left immediately.

The Englishman was neither happy nor sad to see John Cessna. He had very few questions about where Cessna had been taken, what he had seen. He was asked if he planned to go home or wanted a job here. No concern was shown for his well-being or needs.

He was told that a wagon train of furs would soon be leaving for Albany, and he could hitch a ride. But he would have to pay his fare.

As indifferent as the hospitality had been among the Indians, it was warmer than what he now found among his own people.

John appeared to them to be a beggar. He wore haggard clothing and was unwashed. While the Indians freely shared of their food, he was offered nothing by the whites. He was given food, but only if he begged. He found his own place to sleep, but was given no blanket for warmth.

John Cessna was destitute. He had no weapons, tools, or travel equipment of any kind. He had neither money nor anything of value to trade for what he might need.

The clothes he wore were designed for working in the hot July wheat field, not for sleeping on the ground during the cold forest nights. He had nothing.

Eventually, John was able to trade work for warmer clothing. The waggoneers agreed to take him along only if he would exchange work for the price of passage.

John Cessna was responsible to "bed down" the animals at the end of each day's march. And he had to rise before the others, and harness beasts to their burden.

That is how John made his way home: from Johnstown to Albany, Albany to Elizabethtown, Elizabethtown to Reading, Reading to Harris' Ferry.

Always, he had to stay with an armed party that was headed his way. The forest was still too dangerous to travel alone.

Finally, he arrived at Carlisle. It was mid-December.

He had worked his way home, doing the most menial of labor in exchange for food, transportation, and a filthy blanket.

He had never been so desolate in his whole life. During those weeks he never had even one coin in his pocket. It was humbling.

Those long days of having nothing gave John Cessna time to reflect on his life and values. He thought about his modest beginnings in Ireland. Even in the toughest of times, he always had a penny or two. He thought about the poverty of the natives, and how prosperous his own people were.

He thought about his large family, and the many properties he owned and considered himself very blessed. He thought of his escape to freedom and the unlikely way it had happened.

John Cessna realized that he was one of "the favored of God" who were preached about at his church.

John considered the stingy hospitality he was being given. Then he remembered how he had taken advantage of others who were in distress.

The months of travel and denial were freeing for him. Before, he viewed his comforts as something he had earned. He had often raged if he felt he was being denied something he had a right to.

Forever after this long walk, John Cessna, Sr. would view even the slightest comfort given him with humility and gratitude.

One of the dramatic changes that his family noted was that he was always careful to say "thank you" for even the slightest service done for him.

Never again would John expect anything from life, and he was always grateful for every blessing it gave him.

Arriving at Carlisle, John was greeted by Patience with her usual warmth and love. She hardly knew the man.

John was but a ghost of her brother-in-law. She tended to his wounds and offered to mend his clothes. When she surveyed their condition, she knew that repair was hopeless.

Patience insisted that John could not go home looking like a scarecrow. She searched through her husband's clothes for something to give him. They were nearly worn out, but in better shape than what he was wearing.

Then, Patience told him the story of his brother's feud with Daniel Hogan.

John Cessna sat for long hours with his brother at the jail. Stephen and John were not young men any longer.

Though it was less than a year from their last meeting, each man could hardly recognize what remained of his brother.

"I see your nose is still crooked to the left a bit," stated John. "You should know better than to take what isn't yours," he laughed.

A momentary smile came to Stephen's face and he responded with, "I see that mark on your forehead still makes you look like a white-faced heifer."

The older brother had been brought low by his grief and bitterness. John had suffered just as much, but had found a sort of grace and gratitude.

Stephen was angry beyond consolation. Suffering had made John feel grateful. It had made Stephen feel cheated and victimized.

Eventually, they each stopped trying to bring the other to his private place of suffering, and just sat together in silence.

Eventually, they spoke at length about their father. They discussed his dream for their lives and mimicked his advice to them. John had the best impersonation of his French allegories.

John wondered aloud if Jean le Cesne would be satisfied with the start the family was making in America.

"He was always passionate that we find a place to start the family dynasty over. I wonder if he would think this the place," John offered.

"No, he probably would have given up and moved on a long time ago." Whispered Stephen.

"Are you going on?" asked Stephen.

"I reckon I must," said John in a resolute tone.

"I reckon I have had enough," responded Stephen.

John wanted to argue with his older brother. But the depth of his grief was too obvious.

"I've lost all my children but two. There doesn't seem to be much to go one for."

Neither spoke for a long time. Then Stephen ran a thumb inside his wide leather belt.

"I warrant that you should have this now," he said and in the palm of his hand he held a small knife. It was the same short blade they had fought over so many times as boys.

John had not seen it in thirty years and supposed it long perished. Now he knew that his brother had secreted it from him for all these many years.

Just holding it made John feel the presence of his father, and their brother William.

They spoke again about the Frenchman. They discussed his dream for their lives. Imitating his mannerisms, they tried to make each other laugh.

It hurt them deeply that they might have failed their father's dreams for them. What would he think if he should see them now?

On Christmas Eve, John was offered a ride the last twenty miles to Shippensburg.

The woods were still far from safe and it was necessary to wait for an armed party to make this last part of the trip. It would not do for John to have endured so much, only to be killed a few miles short of getting back home.

This group of Shippensburg friends felt heroic about returning a prominent resident to their town.

About 3 p.m., a haggard and weary skeleton of the family patriarch opened the door of the stone tavern on King Street. Every eye turned to inspect the tattered man who entered.

Six-year-old James was first to recognize him, and cry, "Pa!"

The family fell on him in ecstatic joy. The news of his return ran through the town like a Spring breeze.

People began to gather around the tavern to witness this miracle.

It would be five years before John learned the fate of his sons Jonathan and Joseph. After the things he had witnessed, he was more than a little convinced that they must be dead.

CHAPTER TWENTY-THREE
Peace?

The Supreme Council of Pennsylvania finally realized that the colony was at war and began to invest money in defense and trained military.

England began to win the war on most fronts around the globe. The French ran short of money and power. France would lose most of her holdings in the Caribbean because of the war. And eventually, as the English army moved West along the great lakes, they would lose Canada as well.

The tide of war changed with the arrival of Brigadier General John Forbes, the Commander of the British Expeditionary Forces. His army reached Carlisle in the Summer of 1758.

Stephen Cessna would have loved watching the army camped on the square in front of his jail cell. But he had not survived that winter. Though he seemed to be recovering his health, the Sheriff arrived one morning to find him no longer breathing.

Some felt it was the news that another son had died which killed him. Thomas, had perished at the hands of the red savage. This news drained Stephen's will to live.

Thomas had been caught at his farm by another marauding band.

Stephen Cessna, son of the French soldier, died just 10 days shy of his 64th birthday.

Of his four sons and daughter, only Theophilus remained alive. The boy was not yet 17 years of age.

Three grandchildren had been taken to North Carolina by their stepfather. One grandson remained in

Carlisle, with his mother, the widow of Thomas. His namesake, Stephen Cessna, was not yet three years old.

Forbes' expedition was much different than that of Edward Braddock. Forbes listened to the advice of the frontiersmen. And he listened to his Indian scouts.

The General enlisted as many Indian allies as possible. He recruited as many veteran Indian fighters as possible and formed them into skirmish groups. This approach would help keep the savages from springing any ambushes on him.

Forbes had something which Braddock had lacked, adequate maps.

Starting at Carlisle, he spent the summer building a wide and durable road through the wilderness to Ft. Duquesne. Every twenty miles or so, he built a sturdy fortification which would allow him to safely store ammunition and supplies for his army.

John Cessna Jr. was one of many teamsters who were hired to carry those supplies for Forbes' army.

Slowly, carefully, he made his way towards the French fort. The enemy had ample time to watch and assess the strength Forbes was bringing against them.

By the time his army approached Duquesne in September, the Indians had all abandoned the French. Watching Forbes' significant force, they were convinced that the English had already won.

Sensing that all was lost, the French burned their fort and headed down the Ohio River. No battle was required to take the peninsula which would become Pittsburgh.

With the French gone, the Delaware and Shawnee people began to seek peace with the English settlers.

Ben Franklin and the commissioners held a new treaty at Easton, Pennsylvania in October. It was attended by many (but not all) of the tribes responsible for the terror. And they made peace.

The natives vowed they would no longer fight with or for the French during this war. In exchange, Pennsylvania promised it would not build any more settlements west of the Allegheny Mountains.

Neither of these parties kept that promise.

By 1762, Major Robert Rogers and his Rangers had pushed across the Great Lakes and captured Fort Detroit from the French. Canada now belonged to the English. There were no more French soldiers to offer money for English scalps.

Peace finally came.

Thousands of prisoners were released by the Indians all across the frontier. In Carlisle, Colonel Bouquet held a conference and hundreds of captives were returned in a dramatic ceremony.

John was heartbroken when his sons Joseph and Jonathan were not among the white children returned by the savages. There was no news about his sons.

John Cessna received a promotion of sorts that Summer. On his 65th birthday, in August, Agnes presented her husband with a suit of "Gentleman's Clothes." The children insisted that he had earned the gracious life of a "retired gentleman." The community agreed.

He would never again dress for labor in a field or stable. Each morning he adorned himself with the suit, and a complementary air of "sophistication."

The ritual of dressing each day reminded him that he was no longer that half-naked man who had wandered through the forest.

Each morning he carried himself to the pub where the elders met. There they held a daily court of opinion to keep the community and colony in balance.

Frequently, this council of old men arrived at brilliant solutions to the thorniest of the world's problems. But no one ever wrote them down, so the world continued in its troubles.

In the early Spring of 1762, life was beginning to return to normal, and people were breathing easier. John's sons were growing into fine men of the community. John, Jr., Evan, and Charles were well known throughout the county.

In the mass evacuation of the war, many half-developed farms came available in the area around Bedford. With their father's help, John, Jr., Charles, and Evans purchased land claims from those families.

John Cessna also arranged for two of his daughters to have farms next to their brothers. Thomas Jones and his wife Elizabeth Cessna-Jones were partnered with Charles Cessna for a three hundred acre farm. Robert Hall and his wife Margaret Cessna-Hall were partnered with Evans for another three hundred acre farm.

The elder John Cessna was hoping that seven of his children would move together and form a new community. He dreamed that they might even start their own town. They could repeat what he had done in 1739, right here in Shippensburg.

The transportation business had changed dramatically in Shippensburg. Forbes' Road made it possible for wagons to get all the way to Pittsburgh.

Pack horse trains were formed at that new location, not at Shippensburg.

But the bells of the oxen and horse teams pulling the wagons continued to ring throughout the day in their tiny village.

John had chosen one bright spring day to take inventory of the harness and tack in his barn. He was discouraged from doing actual work, but he enjoyed taking inventory.

A shot rang out from the house. John Cessna's heart sank. The war was supposed to be over, but the sound renewed every note of terror he had known. Grabbing an axe, he ran for the house, wishing against life that he had brought a gun that morning.

Skidding to a stop in the cabin door, he was horrified at what he found.

His wife lay prostrate on her rocking chair, with two wild savages standing beside her. His daughters were backed against the stone fireplace in obvious fear.

John looked for a gun. Finding none at hand, he took a firm grip on the axe and prepared for mortal combat.

"John!" his wife screamed. "Our boys are home! Our boys have come home."

Frozen in shock, it took John a long moment to recognize his sons.

Five years had transformed them beyond his imagination. It was more than he could comprehend. But Joseph and Jonathan Cessna stood there in front of him. Their blue eyes were unmistakable.

The old man backed out of the door. Both boys followed. The instant that recognition registered in his eyes, they fell into his arms. Nothing could hold back the tears of joy.

As the group held each other tightly, Joseph turned his face to his father and said, "There's bad trouble coming, Paw."

Jonathan began a nonstop monologue of their five-year exodus. They had been captured by Ottawa Indians -- Chief Mintiwaby, to be exact.

The chief had adopted them. Joseph had become a fine Indian, according to his brother.

In midwinter, the boys had made their escape. They had walked all the way from the River Rouge near Detroit to get home. The tale seemed unbelievable, except that the evidence was here before him.

John's heart was overfilled with gladness. His sons were restored. He had survived the war with his family intact.

He had even managed to turn the dark years into profitable ones, and now held twice the property as he had at the beginning of the war. It seemed that God indeed had chosen John to receive great blessing.

He had always prided himself on being "right" about most things in life. This latest good fortune reaffirmed his wisdom and moral superiority.

His captivity had given John something that few other men had ... certainty. He had emerged from his captivity over-confident with his sense of destiny and his ability to more than overcome any situation.

His time in poverty had transformed him into a man of compassion. The weekly blending of Presbyterian preaching on "predestination," tempered with the spirit of his father, had created in John a man confident that he was supposed to excel in this world.

John Cessna counted himself among the "Elect" whom the preacher rambled on about.

He was freed of the need to have the affirmation of others. He was certain that God had chosen him to be more blessed than the average man.

Joseph warned his father that Pontiac was rallying the tribes for a new war against the English. His information seemed certain, and John began to prepare.

In the Summer of 1763, John did two very uncharacteristic things.

The first concerned his brother's wife.

Patience had lost her husband, her home, and all her children except Theophilus. Thomas' wife had remarried, so Patience and her son were no longer welcome in the home of her daughter-in-law.

Margaret Gallacher-Cessna remarried to James Hamilton, and immediately started another family. Neither she nor her baby survived the birth.

Patience was now caring for her orphan grandson, Stephen, as well as Theophilus. John heard reports of their poverty. He had been convinced another Indian war was upon them.

In 1763, taking a wagon with no escort or weapon of any kind, John Cessna fearlessly traveled the twenty miles of forest road to Carlisle. He convinced those remaining of his brother's family that his prosperity was enough for them all, and he moved them to Shippensburg.

He was driven by the concern that this half of the family might just disappear were he not to "save them."

Before leaving, he escorted Patience to the August Orphans Court, and paid lawyers to make sure all of her husband's affairs; as well as those of her son, Stephen, Jr. were in order.

In those records she told the court that her husband was deceased. She stated that her sons John and Thomas are also deceased, and asked for guardianship of the estate due to her grandchildren: Stephen and John, sons of John; and Stephen, son of Thomas.

Patience Cessna, was the kind-hearted woman who had taken him and John, Jr. to her hearth when his first wife died. Now she was to become a part of his household.

She remained with him until she died.

John's nephew, Theophilus, was treated as he did his own sons. He directed Theo to the farm purchased from Will Campbell. He made sure all financial issues were settled with Campbell for the land's purchase. And Theo would use his uncle's guidance to create a solid plantation just a few miles southwest of Shippensburg.

A second action would shock his children and neighbors.

John became a slaveholder.

In October, John rode from the farm back to the tavern he operated on King Street. It was earlier in the morning than usual. Climbing the steps, he noticed a large pile of rags on the porch. Curiosity getting the better of him, he gave it a poke with his cane.

A high-pitched squeal erupted and two small black faces emerged from the rags. Terrified girls of about 8 and 10 jumped to their feet in apology. John was stunned.

Mrs. Cessna explained that the tavern's guest was Michael Wilkins and his wife. They owned the two Negros, and were making their way back to

Philadelphia. The Indian war had made Mrs. Wilkins change her mind about building a plantation near Fort Pitt, and they were selling out.

John was troubled by the situation. The faces of the girls reminded him of the frightened face of a young blonde girl he had been unable to help. He remembered what it felt like to be a slave to the savages. He remembered his young sons being carried off into slavery.

After two moody hours of drinking, he sent for Mr. Wilkins. John offered him cash for the two girls.

His family was stunned. John had never spoken kindly of holding slaves. He had even refused to accept any indentured help in his service. Yet now he owned two slaves.

The dark-skinned sisters would find a home with the Cessnas. Rather than "owning" them, John considered himself their "protector."

Somehow he felt more justified with this arrangement. They became an intimate part of the household, and their contribution to the work made it possible for Agnes and Patience to assume a more leisurely lifestyle.

Before his death, the two young women were given their independence. Though they appear on tax rolls as his property until shortly before he died, they do not appear among the possessions in his will.

His boys frequently argued with him about the moral inconsistency of owning slaves. John always insisted that the girls "were safer here than on their own."

TWENTY-FOUR
Pontiac's War

In May of 1762, war returned just as Joseph had warned. Pontiac's War.

An Ottawa Chief named Pontiac had convinced the tribes around the Great Lakes that they could not live under English rule. He was angry at the French for giving up so easily. He was trying to convince the tribes that if the Indians kept fighting, the French would return.

Pontiac formed a confederation of tribes in a major war dance ceremony. Fort Detroit was soon under siege. The smaller forts at Presque Isle and Le Boef fell in massacre and fire.

Pontiac was sending war parties back towards Pennsylvania. It did not take long and Fort Pitt and the community of Pittsburgh were under siege as well.

In this war, there was no European nation providing them with weapons or buying scalps. This time, the Warriors did not come to get wealthy. This time they came to release their hatred of the white settlers.

There were not enough Indians to overwhelm Fort Pitt. But when they spread out into the surrounding farms, the war parties killed everyone they could find.

Small war parties were once again slipping through the passes into Central Pennsylvania. Though the raiding and murder never reached the proportions it had in the earlier war, terror returned to the Cumberland Valley.

Pontiac's War was smaller, but still a real war. Pennsylvania was more prepared this time. Fort Pitt was well supplied and though thousands of Indians surrounded it, the army held out well.

The fine road built by General Forbes meant that relief and supplies would not be long in arriving. The line of strong forts which Forbes had built provided safety for the farmers.

War parties still swooped down onto the smaller and more isolated communities. People died, and the western settlers fled in a mass exodus. By July, there were over 1,300 refugees living in Shippensburg. Once again, John Cessna's town was a refugee center.

This time the frontiersmen were much better prepared. The response to each Indian raid was more organized. Fewer of the war parties made it back to their home successfully.

The frontiersmen now knew which passes and trails the Indians would use, and it was easier to "cut them off at the pass."

In March of 1764, for instance, six Indians killed a man and carried five prisoners into the mountains about four miles from Shippensburg. A party of one hundred white men gave immediate pursuit. They soon caught and killed all the savages.

Joseph Cessna had begun to disappear for weeks at a time, wandering the woods somewhere. He would reappear suddenly, and work alongside his father for a day or two, then vanish again.

It was dangerous to wander the woods alone. But Joseph seemed part Indian now.

A man visiting the Cessna tavern one day told a story which explained Joseph's behavior. John and Agnes Cessna were shocked by his tale.

A few weeks earlier, the Indians killed the two Renfrow girls about eighteen miles West of Shippensburg. The girls had left the stockade to fetch some precious belongings from their cabin. They intended their stay to be brief. Their horses were ready to make their escape back to safety.

As John had heard the story, a neighbor had ridden by and warned the girls to leave, but they lingered. Before he was a quarter mile away, he heard shots and knew the savages had arrived.

When he returned with help a short while later, both girls had been killed and scalped at the door of the cabin.

According to the friend relating the story, Joseph Cessna and one of the Girty boys had happened by about that time. They gave chase immediately, even though there were only the two of them and the size of the war party was unknown.

The next day, Joseph Cessna and James Girty returned to find the neighbors burying the Renfrew girls. Without saying a word, they walked up to the grave and laid the girls' scalps on their bosoms.

They also laid the scalps of two Indian warriors on the girl's feet. Then they vanished once more into the forest.

John Cessna would never quite understand the transformation that had befallen Joseph. He was more a creature of the forest than his son.

That Summer of 1763, Colonel Bouquet arrived in Shippensburg with two companies of Scottish Highlanders. The squalling bagpipes and marching troops made an unbelievable sight.

The parade and spectacle the army made was a great encouragement to the frontier people. They were on their way to rescue the people of Fort Pitt who were surrounded by savages.

The Army was here to save the day. Spirits were lifted throughout the county.

On May 16, General Bouquet wrote a letter to his superiors describing the conditions at Shippensburg. He pictured it as horribly over-crowded with refugees filling every home and any building suitable for keeping the rain off. Bouquet was shocked at the level of panic among the people he met.

As Bouquet's army approached Pittsburgh, it was ambushed by a large party of the savages near Bushy Run.

This was actually not a "party" of warriors, but several dozen large war parties which had been dogging the army for many miles. They waited until the army was deep into a thick forest and made a mass attack.

There really was no coordinated leadership among the Indians. This only made a coordinated defense against them all the more difficult. The officers did not know where to expect the next assault.

Not used to fighting in the underbrush, the British soldiers were badly mauled. When night fell, they spent the darkness licking their wounds. It looked like it was going to be another massacre to equal General Braddock's.

But at dawn, Colonel Bouquet roused his troops and ordered them to make a bayonet attack. "Where?" asked the confused officers. The army was completely surrounded by hidden enemies.

"There!" commanded Bouquet, pointing West towards Pittsburgh.

In a crazed effort to turn the ambush from a disaster into victory, the Highlanders simply charged into the woods with a terrifying scream.

Bagpipes turned the morning air into a shrill and horror-producing cacophony.

They ran for three miles, shooting and stabbing any savage they met. Ballads written about the battle said that some of those Indians did not stop running until they got all the way back to Fort Detroit.

The siege of Pittsburgh ended before Bouquet's army reached it. The war lasted just over a year. However, several Chiefs and their warriors continued their war on the English settlers well into the Fall of 1764.

In 1768, Sir William Johnson called a large conference at Fort Stanwix. Following Pontiac's defeat, Johnson convinced the Six Nations to sell all of the land south of the Ohio River to the English.

This gave complete rights for settlement to all of what would eventually become West Virginia and Kentucky. Daniel Boone and others immediately began planning new communities.

There was, however, one profoundly serious flaw in the treaty.

The Shawnee and Cherokee tribes were not invited to the meeting at Fort Stanwix. And they considered this land to be theirs. The Iroquois reasoned that since they had defeated these tribes in battle on several occasions, they had the right to sell their land to the whites.

But the Shawnee and Cherokee did not take kindly to the white men moving into their hunting ground.

Kentucky especially was in contention. The Indians had long fought over its rich hunting resources. After a long and bloody war, the Shawnee and Cherokee agreed that neither of them would live there. But both could use it for their Fall hunts.

Ken-tuk-eee would be a place where all Indians could visit to hunt and feed their families. But none would live there, or claim its exclusive ownership. The last Indian village removed itself from Kentucky about 1710 as a part of this agreement.

When Daniel Boone arrived, he was delighted to find no Indians living there at all.

But the natives returned the next year for hunting expeditions. When they found Daniel Boone living there, they were less than pleased.

Once again, war was inevitable.

No new war needed to be declared. The Shawnee considered the new residents of Kentucky to be trespassers and they felt free to kill everyone they found.

CHAPTER TWENTY-FIVE
Prosperity

1762 and 1763 was a time of accumulating wealth for John Cessna and his sons. Dozens of frontier families were looking to "sell out."

Seven years of war with the Indians had been enough. The thought of another war was too much for many families.

While most people were fleeing the disputed lands around Fort Bedford, the Cessna family made a very daring move and rushed towards them. It defies logic to explain their actions considering what was happening around them.

In May of 1763, John Cessna, Sr. headed for the Land Office in Carlisle. In one pocket he held descriptions of five different farms. They were all adjacent to each other, about thirteen miles south of Fort Bedford.

At that moment, Fort Bedford was under siege from a dozen war parties.

John had acquired these from families who were fleeing the Indians. Either they had no heart to continue, or were desperate for a bit of cash to support themselves in their exodus.

Refugees were selling off their land claims at drastically reduced prices. And they were paying unreasonable prices for the things they needed in their exodus.

John had a store and a tavern. He had a place that could house and feed travelers. He had a hunger for the wealth that land brought. He had lots of spare cash saved up. God was good! Opportunity practically fell at his feet.

At last Edward Shippen began to issue patents for lots and farms that people had been leasing from him. The 25 year contracts were up in 1763.

John Cessna was given title to three lots in Shippensburg. But it was title to land that he had been renting and developing for a long time.

At the Land Office in Carlisle, John purchased Warrants for a number of new farms. They were clustered together.

He was proud of himself. His family was shaping into a dynasty. He hoped his father would be proud of the way things were turning out.

He thought much about his father in those days. He made most decisions based on what the old Frenchman might want.

In 1763, the Cessna Family took a giant step towards moving half of the family. Their plan was to relocate seventy miles west of Shippensburg, to what would become Cumberland Valley Township.

The area they chose was a dozen miles south of Fort Bedford.

On 17 May 1763, John Cessna, Jr. applied for a warrant on three hundred acres of land, south of Fort Bedford, along the Great Road to Fort Cumberland, at the branch of Evitts Creek, including the improvements of Wm. Trent, known as "the Block Houses". The price of the Warrant was £9 per hundred acre and the promise to pay one penny per acre in quit rents for every year until the Patent process was complete. The Block Houses was a private fort built during the last war.

On 17 May 1763, Robert Hall and Evan Cessna jointly applied for 350 acres, including the improvements of Phillip Baltimore and Thomas Jones. The land is thirteen miles from Bedford on road to Fort Cumberland, on Evitts Creek. The price was £9 per one hundred acres and one penny per acre quit rents for every year after. Robert Hall was married to Margaret Cessna, sister of Evan. This was a family partnership.

On 17 May 1763 Thomas Jones and Charles Cessna filed a warrant requesting survey for three hundred acres of land, including improvements of Jones, adjoining Robert Hall and Evan Cissna, on a branch of Evitts Creek about two miles from the block house. The Price was £9 per one hundred acres and 1 penny per acre quit rents every year after that. Thomas Jones was the husband of Charles's sister, Elizabeth. This was also a family partnership.

On 17 May 1763 Jonathan Cessna and Joseph Cessna applied for a warrant and survey on three hundred acres, including their improvements, adjoining James Levingston on the road to Fort Cumberland; at £9 per 100 acres, and 1 penny per acre quit rents for every year after.

Joseph Cessna was only seventeen years old and Jonathan was fourteen. Because both boys were underage it seems their father, John Cessna Sr. purchased it in their name. Their ages also make it unlikely that they were the ones who made the improvements.

On 3 June 1763, Charles Cessna applied for a warrant and survey of one hundred acres known as "Ackney's Bottoms", located next to land known as The Block Houses, belonging to John Cessna, Jr, along the

Great Road to Fort Cumberland. Price was £9 per hundred acres and one penny per acre Quit Rents for every year after.

This made a total of five farms, purchased for seven families. All of the farms were close to each other. Combined, this required a total £197 in cash, paid to the Carlisle Land Office at the time of application for Warrants. More cash was required for the official government survey when it was completed.

None of these couples had the cash to purchase these warrants.

Their father, John Cessna Sr. had been saving for this day. This was to be a dramatic clean start for the Cessna Dynasty.

Homesteads were secured for John and Sarah Rose-Cessna and their children, Jonathan, and Rachel; Charles and Elizabeth Culbertson Cessna; Thomas and Elizabeth Cessna-Jones; Robert and Margaret Cessna-Hall; Evan and Mary Cessna; Joseph and Jonathan Cessna (teenage bachelors).

Many of these couples were young: Charles Cissna, 23 years; Evans, 21 years; Elizabeth, 20; Margaret, 18; Joseph, 17 and Jonathan, 14.

CHAPTER TWENTY-SIX
The Going

A Wagon Train carrying the seven Cessna families left Shippensburg in Mid-July of 1763. They were joined by other families also. William and Edward Rose, Samuel and Robert Culbertson, all brought their own families.

John, Jr. was married to William Rose's daughter. Charles was married to the Culbertson's sister. This was a wagon train made up of extended families.

Bedford was still in the midst of Pontiac's War. It was an extremely dangerous move.

War parties were moving through the area. The people living around fort Bedford had moved into the stockade for safety. None were building new cabins and farms. This group of families from Shippensburg were doing the unthinkable.

John Cessna, Jr. had served with both Bouquet's and Forbes' Armies as a teamster. He had also served for 10 years in the militia. He had experience fighting Indians.

Having lived as an Ottawa Indian for five years, Joseph provided a sense of security. He would serve as scout.

Joseph offered a good deal of insight into the nature of their enemies. He was convinced that the size and strength of this wagon train would discourage most war parties from attacking them.

"The Shawnee and Ottawa will never fight unless they have the advantage of numbers and surprise. You must always be on alert and stay in large groups.

"The Indians value life differently than us," Joseph explained. "The tribe's wealth and strength are measured by the number of warriors it has. Each death is a blow to the entire tribe, so they never expose themselves carelessly. To be killed foolishly would be to rob the tribe of its protection.

"When I ran away," Joseph continued "It was a terrible crime. I was stealing a warrior from the tribe. It was an unforgivable crime. I can never go back."

In the Spring and early Summer, Fort Bedford had been assaulted four times. Each time, the war party had been too small to stage a full-scale siege.

Spreading out into the surrounding countryside, they did manage to kill a number of careless people, and steal one horse.

The Savages had succeeded in terrorizing the people, so much that they were crowded into the fort. These folks were quickly running out of ammunition and food. The situation was getting desperate.

John and Joseph Cessna hoped that their group was large enough to discourage any attack. And though they saw glimpses of war parties, nothing more happened than a couple of horses being stolen from their camp one night.

This changed as they got closer to Bedford. Crossing a small stream as they were entering Aliquippa Gap. They heard gun fire ahead of them.

Within moments, two riderless horses came running down the road toward them.

John and Joseph ordered the others to bunch closer together and the two brothers rushed forward towards the fighting.

In the middle of the pass, at a perfect spot for an ambush, they found two men hiding in the brush. They fired as fast as they could reload. There were at least six warriors firing back at them.

John and Joseph opened fire from a new direction. Faced with two enemies, and being in a crossfire, the savages quickly withdrew.

Jacob Fox had been shot through the leg and was bleeding badly. Thomas Boyd was quick to give the details of their story.

Fort Bedford had been under siege for four straight weeks. In truth, most of the people in the county had fled at first word of Indians coming.

There were now only about forty souls hiding in the fort. Captain Ouray and six soldiers were their only protection.

Ouray had not been able to get a messenger to the army back East. They were isolated without any hope of rescue or resupply. And they were starving.

Fox and Boyd had volunteered to make a desperate trip back to Carlisle, hoping to convince the Army to come to their rescue.

They had not gotten far when they were ambushed. It seemed certain they would die there, until the Cessna brothers turned up.

The Cessna party rushed the last five miles from Aliquippa Gap to the fort. The women immediately began to doctor Fox's wounds.

When their wagon train arrived at Fort Bedford it was greeted with an overwhelming welcome. It had been weeks since any other party had been able to make it through.

The Cessna party represented a kind of relief column for those people hiding in the fort. It was large enough, and had enough men with weapons that the Indians had been afraid to attack their wagon train.

Now the fort had even more men and guns to keep the savages at bay.

The Cessna's were a welcome sight for another reason. The family had come to stay.

They brought with them enough flour and corn meal to last them until the following Spring. They brought with them a dozen muskets, four shotguns and three pistols.

What had been the stores to support their family, now became emergency supplies for an embattled community.

Nine hundred pounds of flour and five hundred pounds of corn meal would feed those huddled in the fort for a long time. It would certainly last until the army could open the roads again.

Without intending to do so, the Cessna family became the rescue party that the Bedford community had been praying for. More fighting men. More guns and ammunition. More food. More horses. And small flock of sheep.

Fresh faces, new stories, and renewed optimism all combined to breathe hope into those folks huddled behind the log walls. The Cessna men were instant heroes, and enormously popular.

With the addition of so many supplies and weapons, the situation turned better quickly for the people at Fort Bedford. They stopped cowering behind the walls.

Charles Cessna emerged as a natural leader for rationing the supplies in such a way that they could feed the much larger crowd.

Charles also organized a system for escorting people who had to return to their farms to save livestock and crops.

Now there were enough men and weapons that they could venture out and resume their lives. Parties were formed to deal with their neglected farms.

In groups, the men took turns performing chores at each other's farms. Three mounted men stayed on continual watch. These were their best marksmen.

Under this protection, six to ten men would harvest the winter wheat, gather livestock, mend fences, and repair doors or shutters broken by the Indians.

By spending just three days at each farm, they were able to save much of each homesteader's yearly labor.

By the end of the first year, John, Charles, Evan Cessna, and their brothers-in-law were familiar with every farm within twenty miles of the fort. They had invested several days of sweat-equity into each of those farms.

And when the Cessnas were ready to erect cabins on their farms, the grateful people all pitched in to help.

Col. Bouquet arrived with his army a few weeks later. He was on his way to relieve the soldiers in Pittsburgh.

But peace was not secured with his arrival. And regular supply trains did not resume until the next year.

Small war parties continued to harass the Bedford folk for the rest of 1763. No one knew when the next attack might come.

Bonding took place in those months of living dangerously. This community became as close as family. Those who joined the community later would be welcomed, but the families who endured the war years of 1763-1764 would always remain special friends. During those years Charles Cessna emerged as impromptu and unofficial commissary. He had a keen eye for how much food and equipment would be needed by the community.

It would take fifty pounds of flour and/or corn meal to last one adult through the winter. Vinegar, salt, turpentine, and yeasts were needed as well as other staples.

CHAPTER TWENTY-SEVEN
A New Community

In 1770, the men of the valleys surrounding Fort Bedford began to cry to the State for recognition. Voices of the Cessnas were among the loudest and most respected. The County of Bedford was organized in January of 1771.

The first elections, reveal how much respect those Cessna brothers held in the community. They were chosen to organize the County.

John Cessna, Jr. and his younger brother, Charles, were chosen for the first Grand Jury of the Quarterly Session Courts. This was the body that determined the county budget and organization. Their first task was to divide the county into thirteen different townships.

Three of the brothers were elected to office in the first round of voting. In the Fall's first election, Evan Cessna was elected as Constable for Cumberland Valley Township.

John Cessna, Jr. was elected as the first Coroner. In the coming decades he would serve eight terms as Sheriff of Bedford County. After that first election, people stopped calling him John, Jr. and referred to him as John Cessna, Esq.

Charles Cessna was elected as the first County Commissioner (the person in charge of making government purchases). Everyone remembered his ability to keep them supplied during the "hard years." His first assignment was to oversee the contracts for building the first Courthouse.

The records of Bedford County's early years are filled with references to the contributions made by various members of the Cessna family. One story which always brought a smile to the family is as follows:

In January of 1776, Jonathan and Stephen Cessna were arrested and charged as being accessories in the jail break of Richard Richardson.

The irony comes from the fact that Jonathan was the older of the boys at 15, and Stephen just 10 years old ... and their father John Cessna, Esq was the Sheriff!

It appears that the boys were trying to help their father at the jail, and inadvertently provided an opportunity for Mr. Richardson to effect his premature release.

Because Richardson was a notorious leader of a Torry gang, the community passion was hot. Loyalty for the Revolution was in question. Their father arrested them and arraigned them before the court. They were acquitted by the Grand Jury and never sent to trial.

John's wife, Sarah Rose Cessna, had more than a few choice words for all three when the ordeal was completed. And John became known as the "sheriff who was so honest that he arrested his own sons."

Hearing how her children were flourishing in far off Bedford, was the last great blessing of Agnes Cessna's life. In the winter of 1771-72 she succumbed to pneumonia. Her husband was devastated.

John Cessna Sr. suddenly found himself with few family allies. Seven of his children had moved seventy miles West. And now he had lost his wife and partner.

The loss of Agnes' guiding spirit was quickly and profoundly felt. The business at the Tavern was under her purview. With his father's depression, 19 year old James Cessna shouldered its administration.

Within a week, John Cessna felt overwhelmed by the decisions that needed to be made. Agnes seemed to manage them easily. John found himself struggling and confused more than he expected.

His life quickly receded into a vague role of supervisor. At the age of seventy-three, he found that he not only lacked the strength but the heart to do most chores.

John Cessna still wandered by and gave instructions to his sons. But they made decisions according to their own wisdom, and not his angry tirades.

CHAPTER TWENTY-EIGHT
Ten Years of Supervising

Eventually, the war was replaced with peace and prosperity. The Cessna siblings settled in on the farms they had warranted in the beautiful valleys and coves around Bedford. A town began to spring up just South of the fort. The road filled with freight wagons and immigrants headed west again.

Money began to flow up and down the road between Harris' Ferry (now Harrisburg) and Fort Pitt (now Pittsburgh).

The economy hit a major setback in 1771. England's Parliament wanted to be paid back for the money spent fighting Indians for 10 years. It taxed the Colonies without mercy.

The effects of the harsher policies were felt in Shippensburg. The amount of money flowing up and down the road to Pittsburgh began to slow. Traders were not investing as much as they had been before. The number of teams and wagons was less each week.

John Cessna Sr. entered a season in which he was only needed as a supervisor. A routine developed for the elderly John to "check-in" at various places throughout the day.

The slave girls received their instructions during his breakfast. They stayed at the farm to avoid exposure to town folk. There was plenty to keep them busy.

After breakfast, he rode into town to check on business.

The farm was only a mile east of Shippensburg, so it was a comfortable ride to the Tavern.

Usually, his visit to the Tavern culminated with an extended stop at the Inn of the Widow Piper. Mid-mornings found the older plantation owners gathering to discuss current affairs.

The young people called this The Council of Opinions, because little seemed to come out of their deliberations except opinions.

John held his place on the *Council of Opinions*. They met daily at the Widow Piper's and digested all of the news of the world. Every one of them was disgusted with the way England tried to run things from so far away.

John had few personal chores to do anymore. Everything was managed by his sons or hired men. So he had plenty of time to take note of the changes taking place in his town.

He could see the problems more clearly now. He just could not do much about them. It was a frustrating stage of life for him.

One day, John Cessna, Sr. learned that his son, John Cessna, Jr. (now titled Esq.) had been elected as the 1775 representative of Bedford County to the Provincial Council in Philadelphia.

His oldest son stopped for a visit on his way to serve in Philadelphia.

The elder John Cessna was impressed with his son's success. But he was too prideful to ever let the boy know he approved.

John Cessna, Esq heard nothing but criticism from his father for the entire visit. Following the legislative session, when he was on his way back to Bedford, he did not even stop for another visit.

CHAPTER TWENTY-NINE
The War for Independence

England was deep in debt from its wars. Sentiment in London bristled that so much money had been spent protecting the colonists from their Indian adversaries. The colonies should pay their share!

Parliament began to pass onerous taxes on those colonies. Before this, taxes had been used to control imports and exports and keep the economy running smoothly.

Now, the clear intent was to move money from the colonies back into the King's treasury. England was draining money from their economy.

No one protested more than the merchants in Boston. Crowds gathered in the street to make frequent and violent demonstrations.

Shippensburg's Council of Opinions spent three full days digesting stories about Boston's Massacre and a certain *Tea Party*. John Cessna, Sr. thought the New Englanders had lost their minds.

Ben Franklin fanned sympathy with frequent stories in the *Pennsylvania Gazette*. One of the rituals of the old gentlemen at Widow Pipers was reading the Gazette aloud to a chorus of emphatic opinions.

General Thomas Gage had been sent by Parliament to "baby sit" the Bostonians, and bring the unruly crowds to order. In April of 1775, he thought of a way to prevent open war.

General Gage did not overlook the growing resentment among the people of Boston. Hoping to head off any real trouble, he sent seven hundred soldiers to seize the arms and munitions of the militia which were stored at Concord.

The government had a number of warehouses with arms and ammunitions, stored at various places around the colonies. These were to be used in case of another Indian War.

General Gage was now worried they might be used to start a different kind of war. Gage did not think it proper that the King's own arsenal might be used against him.

The General badly underestimated how the colonists would respond to having their arms taken away.

Twenty years of Indian wars made them very touchy on the subject of militia supplies. If another Indian War began, they would need those guns. The French may have left the continent, but the Indians certainly had not.

Some of the militia men responded and formed an impromptu army. Fighting broke out and the British regulars were chased all the way back to Boston, losing hundreds of men along the way.

When farmers throughout the countryside heard of the skirmish, they grabbed their rifles and came running.

By nightfall that day, Boston was surrounded by several thousand armed farmers demanding that the Brits leave town. Word quickly went out to all the other colonies for help.

In Philadelphia, delegates from each of the colonies had just gathered and organized the Continental Congress. It had been called into existence to think of a way to negotiate compromise from the King.

Now it found itself declaring war on behalf of all thirteen colonies.

Fearing that the disorganized men around Boston might turn into a destructive mob, the Congress appointed George Washington to be Commanding General and sent him immediately to take control.

Washington had a first request. He asked for a special weapon: an elite fighting force.

George Washington had spent time on the frontier and knew the capabilities of the new rifled gun being used by the pioneers. He also knew what great marksman these farmers had become.

He asked Congress to raise a battalion of six companies of marksmen from the frontier counties. This would give him eight hundred sharpshooters to sting the Brits.

The response was so overwhelming that instead of six companies, nine companies of volunteers were raised. Within 10 days of Washington's request, two companies from Bedford County were organized, equipped, and marching to Boston.

Among them was the orphan, Stephen Cessna. John Cessna, Sr.'s great nephew was now a strapping young man of nineteen, and a remarkable marksman with the rifle John had given him. Stephen and Patience would have been proud if they could see their grandson.

Stephen was the first Cessna to both draw and shed blood for the American Revolution. He served the entire first year of the war, but returned home a changed man. The book *Forgotten Courage* provides a detailed account of his experience with the war.

Cessnas played a part in almost every theater of the Revolutionary War.

But John Cessna, Sr., son of the old French warrior, had grown old. He would be little more than a spectator for this war.

He watched as his sons and grandsons took their parts. He witnessed the people of Cumberland and Bedford counties be transformed from English Colonists into "Americans."

John still held his place on the Council of Opinion in Shippensburg. They met daily at the largest of the taverns and digested all of the news of the war. Every one of them was disgusted with England.

"Remember their solution to the war with the French? They sent a band of pretty toy soldiers over to parade in front of the Indians. I guess they thought the savages would be impressed with how beautiful they were, and just beg for peace." John was cranking up one of his favorite political sermons.

"The woods is full of their bones!" added Will Campbell.

"Now they want us to pay for their foolishness," added Sam Culbertson. "They can't see that they are draining all the cash out of these colonies, and putting our economy in a mess. How can we pay taxes if nobody has any cash?"

Twenty years of watching the English relations with the Indians had turned the old men into great disbelievers.

In March of 1776, Washington succeeded in getting the British Army to abandon Boston. Everyone hoped that this meant Parliament would negotiate with the colonies and things might get back to normal.

Instead, the Army reorganized itself at Halifax and invaded Long Island, across the bay from New York

City. It was now obvious that the war would last for a long time.

In the forts along Western Canada, the English officers borrowed a strategy from the French.

Lavishing gifts on the local tribes, they offered great rewards if they would stage "punishment" raids on the settlements in New York, Pennsylvania, Virginia, and Kentucky.

A new Indian War had begun. The fears of Shippensburg's Council of Opinions had proven prophetic.

The Continental Congress voted to "go for broke" and declared Independence on July 4th.

In 1776, Congress voted on its first military draft. Ben Franklin himself was the architect. It was, for the most part, very humane and considered the needs of the backwoods farmers.

The constable of each township would create a list of all the able-bodied men in their district. The Colonial Assemblies would commission field officers from the most able of the county's leaders. These officers would organize a "Muster" where everyone was incorporated into a newly organized militia.

Regular "Musters" were held for training and organization. The men were divided up into companies and elected their own Captains, Lieutenants and Ensigns.

The captains then appointed Sergeants and Corporals. Each company was divided up into eight "classes." Each class was to be called to serve for two months.

Ideally, each man would serve a two-month tour of duty every 16 months.

The companies were organized of township neighbors. But they were called to service by classes. All men of 1st Class; no matter what company they were assigned to, would serve with the Captain of 1st Company. Their term was for two months.

The class system ensured that only a few from each township were on active duty at any one time.

The plan was that these groups would muster and train together. Then, as help was needed, they would be "called up by classes" to serve for just eight weeks. Everyone hoped the war would be over before they were needed again.

If men chose not to serve, they could hire a substitute or pay a fine. The fine was equal to what it would cost to pay for a substitute.

Those young men eager for a fight (or needing some cash) could and often did hire themselves out to serve in other's places.

This system assured that not too many men from one township (or from one family) would be gone at the same time. The business of the family farm could continue.

Those townships East of Shippensburg would provide units to help General Washington when he needed militia to supplement the Regular Army.

Those townships West of Shippensburg would defend against the Indian war parties.

Ben Franklin was chairman of the Committee of Safety for Pennsylvania. He knew the Cessna family well, as did other men on the Committee.

John Cessna, Esq was promoted to the rank of Major and designated as a Field Officer. Field officers organized all of the battalions in the County, and supervised their training. They administered loyalty oaths to the officers of each battalion and company.

Charles Cessna was also promoted to the rank of Major. He was designated as the Adjutant for Bedford County's First Militia Battalion.

Charles would later be promoted to Lt. Colonel, and also be appointed commissioner to keep these companies in supplies and ammunition.

In the second year of the war, John Cessna, Jr. was elected Sheriff of Bedford County. He filled that office the entire length of the war.

As both a Militia Field Officer and County Sheriff, John Cessna, Esq was responsible to see that the citizens did their militia duty, or paid the fine. One of his first assignments was to confiscate weapons of those who refused militia duty, in the fear they might be Tories.

Congress had ordered that if men would not use their weapons to defend the new government, they should be prevented from using them against it. There were immediate protests as people pleaded that these weapons were needed to protect their families against the savages.

Those mountain passes most frequently used by the Indians were now well known. In the past they usually came in small groups of 4 to 12 warriors.

Charles laid out a careful plan by which each pass would be continually manned by a company of twenty rangers. The idea was to discourage as many war parties as possible.

The rangers would give immediate chase to any who happened to slip through. With Rangers blocking all of the passes, it would be difficult for the war parties to escape with prisoners.

The men of Bedford County took turns serving as rangers for the next five years. Each would serve two months on guard at a pass. Then, hopefully, they would have 12 months off before their next tour of duty.

The Indians continued to send raiding parties, but they were less profitable and more swiftly prosecuted. The system was successful. That is, until the Indians decided to come in larger parties. These frequently outnumbered the ranger companies.

John Cessna Sr. took immense pride in reminding the Council of Opinion that his sons had followed "his advice" in setting up the Ranger Companies. None of his friends believed him.

No one on that council found much comfort as the death toll continued to mount. Widow Piper lost her son James at the Battle of Long Island.

Washington's losses were stunning. But by the end of the war, more lives were lost to fighting savages in the West than by Washington's armies in the East.

On Saturday, July 15, 1780, Col. Charles Cessna suffered the greatest loss of his command. He had ordered a company of men to go to the relief of a terrified group of settlers at Shoup's Fort.

Captain Phillips and nineteen men rushed to the aid of their neighbors, but did not make it. As they crossed over Tussey Mountain near its southern end, they came to the Heater family farm.

Mr. Heater had built his cabin like a fort, with gun ports on every wall. But, not having enough men to garrison his fort, he had abandoned the farm.

Phillips' company sought shelter in the empty house and waited for daylight. The sun gave no comfort for them.

The first to leave the cabin on Sunday morning discovered that they were surrounded by a force of at least sixty warriors. A large war party had discovered their tracks on a muddy trail and followed them to the cabin.

One of the survivors would later tell that two of the men with the Indians were whites. Those men were their Tory neighbors from Bedford County. Some of their friends had turned into traitors.

A four-hour fight broke out. When the Indians set the roof on fire, Phillips surrendered his men. Two Indians had been killed and two wounded at that point. But none of the Rangers was harmed.

Taken prisoner, the Rangers were divided into two groups. Captain Phillips, his son, and eight others were taken to Detroit and sold to the British. After the war they made their way back to Bedford. The ordeal had destroyed the health of each of them.

The other group of ten was not so lucky. Led into the woods with their hands tied behind them, they traveled barely a mile before their captors decided they were too slow.

The ten rangers were tied to trees and at least four volleys of arrows were fired into their bodies. They were scalped and left hanging from the trees as a warning.

Then the warriors headed East again looking for more families to attack.

Colonel Charles Cessna headed the column that came searching for Phillips' company. He chose to bury the bodies where they fell, because the woods were yet full of danger. He was in a hurry to get his men back to the safety of a fort.

It became obvious that the Indians now came in larger groups and the rangers were outnumbered.

And as the council of old men watched, their community began to fall apart. Disagreement was rampant and violent.

About a third of the people were ready for independence. Another third supported loyalty to the King. And another third did not want any part of the war at all.

Neighbor turned against neighbor. The strife was verbal at first, then economic, and finally vigilante in nature. Frustrated persons began to "persuade" their neighbors with the use of threats.

Many of those loyal to the King abandoned their communities and went to fight with the Indians. They reasoned that if they could show the warriors which farms were owned by rebels, their own farms might be spared.

In 1776 John Cessna, Esq, was a member of the assembly which drafted the first Pennsylvania Constitution. Ben Franklin himself was President. They had started the year as the Provencial Assembly. But when the Declaration of Independence was signed, the Provence ceased to exist and the State of Pennsylvania was born.

The state constitution abolished indentured service and prohibited selling, purchasing, or importing slaves. It declared that in February of 1780, slavery was abolished in Pennsylvania. The new law called for all slaves to be freed by 1808, and that any children born to them could not be considered slaves.

All present slaves in the state would be free in 28 years. John Cessna, Sr., had two household slaves. In a paternalistic attitude, he thought he was doing them a kindness by "taking care" of them.

His son Charles, held a Negro field hand to manage his farm while he was "doing business." William did not hold any slaves, but his neighbors, the Culbertsons, held several.

John Cessna, Esq's wife, Sarah, had a personal slave as her housekeeper. And he still voted to outlaw slavery.

Other Cessnas disdained the practices of both slavery and indentured service. The disparity in the Cessna family opinion was a good representation of public sentiment on the subject.

The men of the Cessna family each took their turn of duty with the Militia. Theophilus (son of Stephen) used a surrogate when one tour fell during the month his wife was expecting.

William found himself serving in General Washington's "flying camp" for longer than the two months required. Stephen Cessna hired himself for an extra tour. He was assigned to Washington's army and served for seven months.

And all of the Cessna boys in Bedford completed several tours of two months' service. The original plan was for each man to serve two months out of eighteen.

But as more people left the county, the remaining men were called up more frequently. Their assignment was to camp in remote woodland passes, waiting for Indians.

John, Sr. was proud that two of his sons were command officers, and his son Evans served as Captain of one of the more successful Ranger Companies in Bedford. His son Joseph used the skills learned in captivity with the Indians to protect Pittsburgh as a scout and later by commanding a company of rangers.

John Cessna Sr. was often found bragging to the Council of Opinions how many of his sons were giving heroic service.

He was not pleased with Jonathan, however.

In March of 1776, Jonathan was elected Constable of Cumberland Valley Township in Bedford County. A few weeks later he received his orders to organize the men of his community into a militia.

But Jonathan wanted no part of war with England and especially the responsibility of drafting men to serve.

Jonathan Cessna, having spent five years in captivity with the Ottawa, decided he would rather live in the wilderness than in the midst of a war.

He resigned as Constable and joined a group of settlers headed down the Ohio River. The group chose the Falls of the Ohio as the place to set down roots.

Jonathan Cessna's son claimed that his father built the first house in the town of Louisville, Kentucky. He used the lumber from his boat to build the house.

Jonathan settled his wife Mary Friend-Cessna, and their son William, into a new home. He thought they were far removed from the war.

But the tribes along the Great Lakes had been recruited by the English to make war on every American they could find. This included those Americans who had relocated to Kentucky.

Shortly after Jonathan arrived in Louisville, Daniel Boone rode into the new settlement. He was raising an army of 1000 mounted militia. Every able bodied man was drafted to be a part of it.

Colonel Boone was staging a "punishment raid." He hoped to dissuade the Ohio Indians from any further raids into Kentucky. He planned to cross the Ohio River and burn several villages to the ground. The strategy was to strike first, fast, and hard.

Jonathan was drafted to go with the party. He never returned.

His body was buried in a hidden grave following the Battle of Piqua. It was hidden so the Indians would not violate it.

John Cessna, Sr. had now lost his first child to the war. He was beside himself with grief. The boy who had been kidnapped by Indians in 1757, had finally been killed by them. It hurt him so badly that he stopped bragging to the crowd at Widow Pipers.

CHAPTER THIRTY
March to Camp

At the close of the year 1776, Washington sent another desperate plea to congress. The enlistments of most of his soldiers were ending the first week in January. His men wanted to go back to their families.

This was especially true for those men from Western Pennsylvania. For months, they had been receiving letters about the murder raids being done by Tories and Indians.

They were deeply concerned that they needed to be home protecting their families. And they were needed!

Pennsylvania decided to send one company of militia from each battalion in the state. They were to serve their two month duty with Washington. This would inflate his troop strength and give him time to enlist and train replacements.

In Bedford, Capt. Jacob Hendershot's company was just organizing their two months of service. Col John Piper ordered this company to march as soon as possible to meet Washington at his camp, and once there, to stay for two months.

Word spread quickly around the county. As Hendershot's men were getting ready, volunteers began to come forward.

Captain Joseph Paxton's company had just completed two months of service guarding the remote passes. They were supposed to have the next 12 months free from military duty.

Capt. Paxton stepped forward to serve an additional two months. Among his company, these men also volunteered for extra service; Lt. Levi Linn, Pvt Cornelius Troax (Truax), and Pvt Joseph Troax, Lt. Moses Reed, Obediah Stillwell, and Lt. John Stillwell. Their nephew Stilwell Troax volunteered for the extra duty as well.

And to the surprise of many, Lt. Col James Graham, Major Edward Coombs, and Major John

Cessna volunteered as well. These officers all volunteered to march with no pay, serving as privates under Captain Hendershot.

Graham, Coombs, and Cessna were Field Officers. They were not assigned to any combat battalion because of their age. So they had no active responsibilities keeping them in the county.

Major John Cessna would turn 51 years old, three weeks later. It would be an exceedingly difficult march for him.

The weather that year alternated between thaws, hard freezes, and heavy snowstorms. The roads were a sloppy and icy mess. The men slept on frozen ground some nights and on soggy ice-cold ground on other nights.

Private Joseph Troax died on February 15, after reaching Washington's camp.

On their march, Major John Cessna insisted that they stop in Shippensburg to rest and get a hot meal at his father's Tavern on King Street.

Major John explained to his father that he had spent two weeks in Bedford County seizing the guns of those who refused to accept militia duty. He was taking these to Washington's army.

"If they won't use them, Washington's men surely can."

It made John, Sr. cry to see his son and these young men making such a difficult journey. Their sacrifice was inspiring. He remembered his own season of hardship and loss.

The Council of Opinions agreed. And the small town of Shippensburg was roused from its winter slumber. The town filled another wagon with supplies for the army. John and James Cessna offered a dozen kegs of whiskey and several hundred pounds of smoked bacon and pork.

The company from Bedford would not arrive at Washington's Camp without bringing food and weapons which the Army needed badly.

Traveling was nearly impossible that winter. The days would thaw, the nights would freeze. Snow was not deep, but the continual thawing and freezing made the roads a painful gauntlet.

Decades later, Private John Peck, a member of Hendershot's original company, filed an application for Revolutionary War Pension. His pension application tells the story of this company's service.

"On this 10th day of March AD 1834, John Peck, a resident of Providence Township; aged seventy-six years; who being duly sworn doth on his oath make the following.

That he entered the service of the United Sates under the following named officers & served wherein stated. That in December of the year 1776, he with about 26 or 27 men marched from Bedford County as volunteers under Major John Cessna, Maj. Combs, Col Grimes & Captain Obadiah Stilwell & proceeded through Shippensburg, Carlisle, Harrisburg & Lancaster, Penn, to Philadelphia & from thence crossed the Delaware for the purpose of joining the regular army; and passed up through New Jersey to Trenton where they arrived a short time after the battle. From Trenton they marched to Princeton where a battle had also been fought a few days before their arrival. That after they came to Princeton they were taken under the command of General Putman and remained at Princeton in Winter Quarters.

Hendershot's company and the volunteers marched to meet Washington in January of 1777. At the time, Washington was just making his Winter Camp at Princeton, New Jersey.

Major John Cessna and the other officers served for two months as privates under command of General Putman. They marched in training. They took their turn as guards on the roads and around supply houses. They even stood watch on the heights overlooking the British Regiments who were camped just across Stony Brook Creek.

When Col Piper reported this expedition to the Safety Committee, he requested that the Pennsylvania Supreme Executive Council authorize pay for the officers and Paxton's men who had volunteered to serve at no pay. They were granted pay from January 9th when their march began, until March 25th when they returned to Bedford.

At Philadelphia, on February 13, 1777, Captain Bickman was directed by the Safety Committee to *pay Maj. Coomb (sic) £75, ten shillings, 6 pence as subsistence for himself, Maj. Cisna (sic), a Captain and 23 men of Col. Woods Battalion from Bedford County.* This draft was not for pay, but money needed to feed themselves.

CHAPTER THIRTY-ONE
The Cessnas Stayed!

The records are clear that a lot of the people living West of Carlisle abandoned their homes and went back to former homes, East of the Susquehanna.

However, the Cessna family stayed.

Just as they had during the French and Indian War, the Cessna family did not abandon one single farm or run from the danger. In fact, every able bodied man in the Cessna family found his way into service either through the local militia or in service to the Continental Army.

The following is a partial list of John Cessna, Sr.'s sons, grandsons, and nephews who served between 1775 and 1783. It is taken from Rolls of the Militia in the Pennsylvania Archives.

John Cessna, Jr. was appointed as a Major and assigned to the Field Officers over all of the militia battalions in Bedford County.

Stephen Cissna, son of John's cousin, Thomas, was the first from the family to volunteer. In June of 1775 he marched with Col. Thompson's Battalion of Riflemen to support Boston. In January of 1776, this Battalion became the very first unit enrolled in the Continental Army; The 1st US Infantry. Discharged in June 1776; days before the tragic Battle of Long Island, Stephen returned to Shippensburg and married.

For the remainder of the war he served numerous times in the militia company from Hopewell Township of Cumberland County. He is recorded as receiving pay for serving as "a Seven-Months-Man" which was a short term enlistment with the Continental Army. This means that he served for two enlistments in the Continental Army.

Charles Cessna was named Major and Adjutant of 1st Battalion of Bedford County Militia in 1776. In 1777, this unit was changed to 2nd Battalion and Charles was promoted to Lt. Colonel. He continued in this rank and position through 1783. Throughout the war he also served as one of the County Commissioners, responsible for collecting taxes and purchasing the supplies needed by all militia companies. He was three times elected as State Representative.

Capt. Evan Cessna, lead Company 3 of the battalion commanded by Charles. For the entire war, he was captain of this ranging company. His duties were to patrol the remote mountain passes, and give pursuit when an Indian attack occurred.

Capt. Joseph Cessna, who had been a captive of the Ottawa for five years, had relocated to Westmoreland County before the war. Joseph served most of the war as captain of a ranging company for Col. Broadhead. He also served a number of months as a scout; moving alone throughout Ohio (enemy territory) to discover the movements and plans of the savages.

Jonathan Cessna, is the other son who was held captive by the Ottawa. Jonathan served a brief period early in the war as a Constable in support of his brother, Sheriff John. He served for two years in the Ranging Company of Capt. Evans Cessna. In 1780, Jonathan and his wife, Mary-Friend Cessna, were part of an exceptionally large party migrating down the Ohio River to settle in Kentucky. This was not a move to a safer place, but to a much more dangerous place.

Shortly after he arrived at Louisville, Jonathan was drafted by Col Daniel Boone, Col Simon Kenton, and General George Rogers Clark, to be a part of a one thousand man army launching a punishment raid into the Shawnee Towns in Ohio. Jonathan was killed on August 8th at the Battle of Piqua.

Capt. Theophilus Cissna, youngest son of Stephen and Patience Cessna, served in several positions in the militia company from Fannett Township. He was promoted from Private, to Ensign, to Captain of a company of rangers. At one point he served as the Captain of the Ranging Company for Northumberland County. Cumberland was sending men to help those counties who were desperately short of fighting men.

Theophilus had three sons who also served. **Thomas** served with his father in the Ranging Company for Northumberland County. **Stephen** and **Theophilus Jr**. served in the militia company for Fannett Township.

Lt. William Cessna served in the militia company from Letterkenny Township, commanded by Capt. Joseph Culbertson. He served several tours of duty. The frequency of his service suggests he may have hired as a substitute for other men. On one enlistment his company was incorporated into Washington's Flying Camp. This last was during the period that Washington was camped at Valley Forge. The Flying Camp, however, was not at Valley Forge.

James Cessna is recorded as a part of the militia company from Hopewell Township of Cumberland County. He mustered several times with his cousin Stephen Cissna (above). James was also terribly busy running the Cessna business in Shippensburg and taking care of his father, John Cessna, Sr.

Major John Cessna had two sons who also served in Bedford County Militia. **Jonathan Cessna** (born 1760) mustered several times with his uncle, Captain Evan Cessna. And **John Cessna Jr**. (born 1764) served in 1783 as a private in the Company of Capt. John Ritchey from Colerain Twp.

Because the Indian War continued long after the surrender of the British at Yorktown, most of these men continued to serve in militia units until well after 1790.

CHAPTER THIRTY-TWO
Ten Year Reign From The Porch

After the British surrendered at Yorktown, John Cessna, Sr. surrendered as well. At the age of 82 he retreated to his farm in the shadow of South Mountain. He ruled his universe from either the chair on the front porch at his farm, or on the porch of the Cessna Tavern.

The two slave girls ministered to his every need. They pampered him and catered to his every whim as though their lives depended on it. And in exchange, they were exempt from nearly all other responsibilities.

The Revolution officially ended in 1783. But real peace was still illusive. Fighting with the savages continued throughout the Ohio Valley.

The most vicious (though not bloody) fighting broke out between neighbors and brothers as the new United States began to pull itself apart from within.

The people began to separate themselves into political parties and soon developed bitter rivalries. Men who once had been friends and comrades-in-arms, now became bitter enemies. John Cessna's sons became embroiled in the conflict.

On an unusually warm afternoon in late February of 1783, John Cessna, Sr. sat on his porch at the farm. His tired body was soaking up the sun while his mind was dancing with memories.

On the distant roadway a lone figure on horseback emerged from the forest. John thought the man looked incredibly sad from his posture.

As the rider grew closer, he recognized the man as his son, Charles. He was surprised because Charles was supposed to be in the state congress at this time.

The girls produced another chair and a mug of cider as Charles dismounted. The son drug himself to a place beside the old man. Instantly, tears filled his eyes and his voice failed him.

John was overwhelmed at Charles' fallen spirit. He knew he should offer comfort, but could find no words. The two sat in a painful silence for long minutes.

Charles was facing the most devastating moment of his life. He desperately wanted to talk to his father one more time.

"It's a mess, Father." Charles finally heaved as his tears began to fade. "It is the worst mess I have ever seen anyone make of themselves."

John Cessna sensed that it was best to stay silent and let the younger man talk.

"I have been expelled from the Assembly, thanks to that Damned George Woods! How I regret that I once saved the man's life. And now he has destroyed mine!"

Charles spent the better part of two hours telling an ugly tale of politics. And it was soon clear that this was only the beginning of the storm which was coming upon him.

During the election in Bedford County the previous Fall, George Woods had brought charges against Charles Cessna. They were rumors at first, then petitions and letters.

Woods charged Cessna with forgery and perjury regarding the way he managed money as the County Purchaser during the war. There were many people still bitter about how things were done during the war.

Charles explained how a packet of receipts had been lost. It represented £160 of government money used to buy food for the militia. He was responsible for it.

"There is no way I could just make up that money personally. I had already lost too much with the worthless currency they were giving me to buy supplies."

Charles paused for a long moment as though about how to confess a terrible sin.

"So...I just made up new copies of the receipts that were lost. Noone but I would know anyway."

"Woods must have found those first receipts. He brought Friedigut and a couple of others forward to claim that they had never been paid for their grain. He charged that I had forged the documents I sent to the state for reimbursement.

"Father, the man stood on the courthouse steps and called me a 'Thief'! And I once saved his life!"

Charles Cessna still enjoyed much popularity among the Bedford County folks. In spite of the accusations, he and George Woods were nearly tied for the office of State Representative. Woods had only a half dozen more votes.

As was custom, both men were recommended to the Supreme Council. Because a fellow Bedford County man who was on the Council preferred Cessna; Charles had been chosen for the office over Woods. The Supreme Council had a right to do this, but seldom did they override the reports of the election judges.

In January, The Honorable Charles Cessna marched in the installation parade through Philadelphia and took his seat for his third term as a State Representative. But that seat would have no chance to get warm.

George Wood had also made the trip to Philadelphia. On Monday, February 17, 1783, Woods stood outside the door of the Supreme Council demanding that the petition and testimonies be presented to the President of the Assembly.

John Piper of Bedford County, and John Dickenson the President of the Council did their best to avoid doing so, but were finally compelled. Three days later, the charges were read to the assembly.

Immediately, the State Assembly voted to remove Charles Cessna from his post representing Bedford County. They then voted to request that the Attorney General should investigate the case.

George Woods was immediately given the seat Cessna vacated.

A week later, an embarrassed and defeated Colonel Charles Cessna, ex-state representative, rode in shame up to his Father's porch. His world was shattered. He was beyond consolation.

"Can we just pay back the £160?" asked John.

"It is not that simple. If I falsified those receipts, how can I prove that none of the others were falsified. All of the thousands of pounds of government money I spent are now in question.

"At the very least, I could be made to forfeit the £500 that was posted as my surety for the post," Charles continued.

"My brothers John and Evans are responsible for that because they posted bond for my service. I can't let this destroy them financially."

"Father, I fear I am about to lose everything. And it is not just my property that I could lose. My brother's, could lose their farms as well."

The mess he was in was overwhelming. How quickly things had changed. One day, he was honored as a hero. The next day he was expelled as a criminal.

They sat silently for a long time. Each man searching soul and mind for any solution.

When the descending sun first touched the crest of North Mountain, the two girls ushered the men to a roaring fire they had prepared inside. Mugs of cider were refreshed as well.

The cider helped his mind bridge the gap of time. At several moments during the afternoon, John felt as though he could hear the Old Frenchman guiding his thoughts.

"My mother once told me a story about the Old Frenchman" John started.

"On the day she first saw him, he was the most pathetic sight she had ever beheld. He rode a broken-down plow horse and wore an elaborate French Cavalry uniform that was little more than threads."

John was now completely lost in his memories and could almost hear his mother's voice.

"She thought it most comical that he had not one single silver button left on his uniform" John chuckled, "having sold them one at a time to feed himself.

"Even the Ostrich plume in his cap was broken and matted. He was 'wee more than pride and rags' she used to say. But he wasn't defeated!"

"Something in that Old Frenchman intrigued my mother. He had been betrayed by both the King of France and the King of England. He had been abandoned in Ulster with next to nothing. He was alone, abused, and ashamed, she used to say. But he wasn't broken."

"Somehow, that Old Frenchman started his life over. With nothing but his spirit and stubbornness, he carved out a new life. He made a new life that he could be proud of.

"Mother used to say, this unbroken spirit is what impressed her most about him. That and his blue eyes!" John added with a laugh.

Those same blue eyes were now looking at Charles from his father's face. They sought to give their son something to hope in.

"I never thought much about that," John went on. "Until that day the Indians came.

"I went from being rich, to a penniless slave in the space of a tomahawk drop. I went from being smarter than all my neighbors, to the dumbest man in town. All in the blink of an eye.

"When I finally got free of them, I had nothing but the torn clothes on my back. People thought I was some kind of traitor; and hardly anyone had pity on me.

"I walked all the way home having to steal most of what I ate. I even stole a blanket from a horse to keep warm. What kind of a man steals from a horse?

"But I learned something on that walk. I learned something that changed me. Remember, I was not walking towards a warm homecoming.

"I was coming to tell Agnes that I had lost two of her sons to the Indians. Try walking towards that kind of a homecoming."

John now got so choked up he had to stop his narration.

"On that journey I learned that the Old Frenchman walks inside of me.

"I learned that the best thing he gave me was the ability to face anything, and still keep going. Cessnas get knocked down. They may even be broken.

"But there is something in the Cessna soul which won't give up. Hell, starting over again with nothing, is sort of what we do best!

"I don't know how you will work all of this out, son. But I know that the Old Frenchman walks inside of you too.

"I know you have the heart and soul of a Cessna. I know you will find a way to walk out of this mess. That is what being a Cessna means. We always have, we always will."

Charles Cessna left his father's farm, feeling a little less defeated. He broke the news to his brothers. Together they decided on their next move.

Col. Charles Cessna, decided he would forfeit the 300-acre farm and the bulk of his livestock to settle any money owed the people of Pennsylvania. And he would quit the state.

Governor Oglethorpe and General Nathaniel Greene had both written letters of encouragement to Col. Cessna. They offered him a fresh start in Georgia where veterans were being given Head Right Grants of free land.

In the Autumn of 1783, Charles moved his family to newly opened land in Greene County, Georgia.

The Carlisle Gazette ran this advertisement *29 Mar 1786, Sale of Plantation, and late property of Charles Cessna Esq, in Cumberland Valley, on Great Road from Bedford to Cumberland. Three hundred acres: apply to Thomas Coulter, Esq near premises; George Funk in Bedford, or Thos Smith, James Hamilton, or Thos Duncan in Carlisle.*

Evan was just as disgusted with the politics of Bedford County. That same Fall he moved his family to Pittsburgh and opened a tavern there.

In 1784, Joseph Cissna, the Indian Fighter, quit the United States. He led a large party of unhappy settlers to live under British rule near Detroit.

John Cessna, born in Ireland in 1699, had now lost three wives; one son to the Indians; and three sons to the political storm that gave birth to this county.

CHAPTER THIRTY-THREE
Five Years of Loss

From the close of the war in 1783 until 1788, John Cessna was continually saying "Goodbye." First Patience, then Agnes, then Margery had faded from this realm into the next.

His friends began to die in rapid fashion, and by 1788, he was the last living person who had come with their group from Ireland. He was ninety years old.

His children and the children of his friends were well-rooted in the new country.

He watched as his wealth was diminished by the economic recession which followed the war. He watched his savings evaporate as Colonial paper money became increasingly worthless.

He began to lose his eyesight, and his hearing. He lost the ability to walk the mile from his farm into town to sit at the Widow Piper's. John was not even able to climb atop his horse any longer.

The Widow Piper was long gone too, as were all of the Committee of Public Opinion.

In the first census of the United States, held in 1790, James "Scisney" is listed as the head of the household. His father, two boys under the age of 16, five females and two slaves made up the family living at the farm beneath South Mountain.

John had lost nearly all of his physical power. He had to be "managed" like one of the livestock. All of his daily needs were chores for the two Negro girls. The only power he was able to retain was his signature.

James could do nothing with the properties without John's signature. The slaves could not leave without his signature.

The attention of the two slave girls kept him alive for years longer than he might have on his own.

John had set each of his sons and daughters up with farmsteads. At the age of ninety he worried if he had succeeded or not.

John's children moved away, needing him less. Cessna watched as his family began to break apart. Jonathan had been killed fighting Indians in Kentucky.

Evans abandoned his farm in Bedford and moved to Pittsburgh where he opened a tavern. In Pittsburgh, such places were primarily for drinking and vice.

John did not approve of his son's business practices. It was not the way Evan had been raised.

Joseph shocked his father with a move back to the forests of Detroit where he had lived as a captive of the Ottawa. Joseph had led a group of disheartened Americans to live under British rule at Fort Detroit. But to his father, Joseph had "gone back to the Savages."

Charles had run into political trouble. He packed his family and moved to Georgia. William eventually took his family and went there as well.

It made no sense to John Cessna, Sr. It just made no sense.

John, Jr., and his sons were spending all of their time in Bedford and seldom came to see the old man. Actually, John, Jr. was calling himself John Cessna Senior, Esquire these days; and the grandson had become John, Jr.

The old man had so many grandchildren and great-grandchildren that it was confusing to him. The girls were married off through the years.

Mary Cessna married Thomas Neale who owned several farms north of Shippensburg. She had married well.

Margaret married Robert Hall and the youngest daughter Elizabeth married Thomas Jones. Neither lived very long after their marriage,

His youngest child, Theophilus, was given a farm in Franklin County, but had yet to show much interest in settling down. Theophilus was a bit of a problem.

Feeling spry at the age of seventy-five, John Cessna, Sr. took a third wife, Margery Palks. It was a brief marriage. The only son of their marriage was born in 1775, just as the country was entering the revolution. Theo's mother had died soon after.

Because of the circumstances, and their age difference, Theophilus never really bonded with his older brothers. He had no real family support.

Theophilus was raised by James with his seven children. But because John was his father, it created many awkward moments for who had the final say on the boy's punishment. The boy, therefore, had little discipline.

Only James remained close with the old man. They were business partners in various enterprises around Shippensburg.

It was not that John, Sr. and James were all that close in their mind set. John was able to hold onto James with the "promise" of inheritance. James was his old age insurance. John had not planned to live so long that James would be an old man.

CHAPTER THIRTY-FOUR
A Last Visit

An event in 1791 provided John Cessna, Sr. a last brief reunion with his son, Major John Cessna.

James Nugent and Thomas Dugan were two notorious criminals from Cumberland County. There were wanted posters hanging up and down the great road leading through Carlisle to Pittsburgh.

Word came to Sheriff John Cessna that these men were hiding out in his jurisdiction. John organized a posse and tracked the men down. When he had been arrested, and placed them in the Bedford Jail, he received a request to transfer them back to Carlisle.

The Quarterly Sessions Court for Cumberland County recorded the request of John Cessna to be reimbursed for his expenses.

The invoice he submitted states: *Account of John Cesna, late Sheriff of Bedford County for bringing down James Nugent & Thomas Dugan of Carlisle. Includes breakfasts, dinners, whiskey, hay, mead, corn, victuals and three men of a guard with horses for 8 days.*

Evidently, it was acceptable to drink while on duty as a Sheriff's deputy in those days.

From this episode alone we can tell a great deal about John Cessna, Esq, the man.

Even at sixty-six years of age, he was capable of hard travel through back country. He knew how to navigate the back woods. And he was not afraid of a challenge, or dangerous men.

It was a ninety mile journey on horseback from Bedford to the Cumberland County Jail.

The trip to Carlisle in 1791 was the last visit Sheriff John made to see his father. He stopped in Shippensburg and found his father at the farm.

Now in his nineties, John, Sr. was a withered version of his former self.

On every such occasion in the past, the visit between father and son had ended in an emotional disagreement. This time, John, Jr. felt no need to contradict anything his father said. He felt no need to present any part of his life in an effort to win his father's approval.

The old man was still coherent. But his memories were crowding his present mind so greatly, that he had trouble focusing. There were moments when he confused past with present facts.

John Cessna, Esq was grateful that his father was being well cared for.

A granddaughter in her young teens provided entertaining company for the ancient man. He was especially fond of her.

Elizabeth was the daughter of William and Margaret Cessna. John, Sr. would make a special bequest to Elizabeth in his Will, out of gratitude for her companionship in his latter years.

He was a little bitter that his own children were neglecting him.

A typical day for the 93 year old man was sitting in a sunny spot, where, in between naps, he could keep track of the people moving up and down the road.

It brought excitement to his tired heart to see what was passing through his town, and who was calling at Widow Piper's Tavern.

Though way beyond having the physical ability to manage his affairs, the elder Cessna still had a keen mind and memory.

In 1791, Sheriff John's three youngest brothers still lived under their father's dominating supervision. Theophilus, William and James lived on properties their father owned and controlled. But it was their labor which made those properties function.

CHAPTER THIRTY-FIVE
Five Helpless Years

The former slave girls got John Cessna up in the morning, and carried him to a sunny place on porch. They made sure he was fed and kept clean. The youngest of the girls slept near him at night. The old white man was the closest thing she had ever known as a father.

There was a strained but honest love between the man and these girls. He was their protector in a new way now. Caring for him ensured they were not given other duties. "The old Mr. needs such and such," was an instant excuse from any request for hard labor.

John had set each of his sons and daughters up with farmsteads. Now in his nineties he wondered if he had been successful or not.

In the fall of 1993, John Cessna had finally worn his body out. On October 22, he gathered his assets and wrote out his will.

To each of his children he gave five shillings (about $1). He had given each of them farms to establish them in life, and this was their inheritance.

John made an extensive list of the other properties he had accumulated. He gave all of this to his son and partner, James.

It was an impressive list of his life's accomplishments. Having come to this country with nothing, his parting possessions included:

1. A certain quantity of backlands taken up and surveyed in partnership with Messeurs Hutton and Wallace.

2. House and lots in Shippensburg, a tract of land in Southampton twp. bounded as described in a conveyance from William Campbell.

3. A tract of land warranted and surveyed along the Juniata creek or river, above Jack's Narrows, now in Huntingdon County.

4. A five shilling warrant taken out from the Proprietary's Office for an island in Juniata River, and another for an older right of it, the said warrant was renewed and laid on the land adjoining the river, including the land where Prigmore's Mill is now built.

5. Also a grant of land got from Mr. Blunston's, lying near the Susquehanna River, on the west side in York County, near Conewago Creek, and adjoining the same about a mile west from the River joining on the Branch of Dry Inlet.

6. Piece of land warranted and surveyed adjoining Robert Gabney's on the south, and land of Samuel Culbertson, purchased from Nathaniel Wilson.

The two possessions he prized the most -- the Huguenot Bible and his father's silver cross -- had perished in 1770 when the stone building on King Street burned down.

Following his father's death, James would run the following ad. It ran every two weeks for almost a year. James was ready to retire himself.

1797-02-08 Carlisle Gazette, Carlisle, PA
To be sold by Private Sale, and may be entered on the first day of April next, a valuable corner house in Shippensburg, on the South-East corner of King Street, and Earl Street, in the most public part of the Town, has been occupied as a Tavern, and part of it now is occupied as a Store; also a good dwelling house in the East end of the town on King Street; also, a lot, near the town well, where a Stone House has been burned down; likewise a tract of nearly 190 acres of good land, about one mile from the Town, about one half cleared, the other under good timber, which will be sold together, or in small divisions, as may suit the purchaser—Terms will be made easy. For further particulars enquire of James Cessna in said town. –James Cessna, Shippensburg, Jan 30th, 1797.

All of the people John Cessna Sr. knew during his active years, had long since passed or moved on. It is a sad thing to outlive all of the people who once respected you.

In his final days, John looked back on all that he had seen and experienced. He wondered if his father would be pleased.

He wondered if his father had expected it to take so many years of war to win this new land. He wondered if his grandchildren would remember the struggle he faced to give them this new life.

He remembered his father's speeches regarding a new beginning for the family. He wondered if it had happened yet.

At age 97, John Cessna died in his sleep the last day of September in 1796. He had no great disease and nothing greater than the aches of old age. He died certain of his favor with God, as evidenced by all of the blessings he had been given.

If his grave received a lasting memorial or stone by his children, it has not survived in any records.

At his last breath, the Coming to America ended. The journey was complete. The Cessna family was very much a part of American's foundation.

ADENDUM
The Land Rush of 1763

The Players:

    John Cessna Sr (the Elder), born in Ireland 1699. Son of the Frenchman

    John Cessna Jr, son of John Cessna Sr. later known as Major John Cessna, bn 1726.

    Evan Cessna, son of John Cessna Sr., bn 1742.

    Charles Cessna, son of John Cessna Sr., bn 1740,

    Thomas Jones, son in law of John Cessna Sr., husband of Elizabeth Cessna, bn 1744

    Robert Hall, son-in-law of John Cessna Sr., husband of Margaret Cessna, bn 1745

Steps to owning land in Bedford County.

1. Squatting or taking a Warrant.
2. Possessing land and making improvements.
3. Paying to have the Warrant Surveyed by Government Surveyor
4. Government Land Office issues a Patent. Some owners waited 100 years or more before applying for patent.

1763: At the end of the French and Indian War, Ottawa Chief, Pontiac, organized a multi tribe war on the English Settlers. On May 16, General Bouquet visited Shippensburg and reported that it was overrun with refugees fleeing the invading war parties. He reported that many of these settlers were ready to "sell-out" and head back East. In the next three weeks, the Cessna family will purchase FIVE large farms in Cumberland Valley Township (which will become Bedford County).

The following land transactions were found in the Quarterly Series: "St. Clair's Bedford: The History and Genealogy of Bedford County, PA. In some cases, micro-film of the original Land Warrants we found on Ancestry.com.

FARM ONE: 17 May 1763, Jonathan and Joseph Cessna (sons of John Cessna Sr) requested a warrant for 300 acres, including some improvements, adjoining James Livingston, on the road to Fort Cumberland. Joseph was age 16 and Jonathan was 13. They paid £27 for the 300 acres, and pledged 12 shillings 6 pence in Quit Rents to the Government for every year there-after. Land was along Evitts Creek at the point where Rome Creek joins it. Livingston's property was to the North of this farm.

On 17 March 1768, Christian Eversole filed a Caveat against Jonathan and Joseph Cessna, stating that this farm is actually in the state of Maryland and he held a patent on it.

FARM TWO: 17 May 1773; Robert Hall & Evans Cessna of Cumberland Co, applied for Warrant on 300 acres, including improvements of Phillip Baltimore and Thos Jones, 13 miles from Bedford on Road to Fort Cumberland on Evitts Creek in Cumberland County. Another reference says Robert Hall bought this land from William Coulter in March 1763. For the Warrant, they paid £27, and pledged 12 shillings 6 pence per year in Quit Rents to the government.

On 21 Nov 1766, Robert Hall sold his half of land 350 shared with Evan Cessna to John Cessna, Sr (his father in law.) Land bordered property of Thomas Jones and Charles Cessna. Sold for £40. Joseph Cessna and Evan Cessna witnessed.

On 28 July 1783: John Cessna Sr granted (no sale price) his share of 350 acres to Evans Cessna, his son.

FARM THREE: 17 May 1763, Thomas Jones and Charles Cessna of the county of Cumberland warranted 300 acres, including improvements, adjoining Robert Hall and Evan Cessna, on the branch of Evitts, Creek, about two miles from the Block House in county of Cumberland. Thos Jones had already made some improvements to it. Price of Warrant was £27. And pledge of 12sh 6p per year in Quit Rents to the government.

In, 11 July 1776, Charles and wife Elizabeth of Cumberland Valley, sold to Thos Farris of same place, price of £200, 235 ½ A. in Cumberland Valley, bordered by Thos Jones and Cessna's other land.

FARM FOUR: 17 May 1763, John Cessna Jr, applied for warrant of 300 acres in Cumberland Valley, land of Wm Trent, known by names of the Block Houses. Warrant cost £27, and pledge to pay 12sh 6p in Annual Quit Rents to the Government. (John Jr is 37 years old, married three years with a 2-year-old and 6-month-old daughter, and wife was pregnant).

On 4 Mar 1766, Samuel Finley bought 200 acres from John Cesna Jr, adjoining land of Charles Cessna, the improvements of William Kirkpatrick, & land of Wm Trent, known by the name of The Block Houses on both sides of Evitts Creek in Cumberland Co.

FARM FIVE: 3 June 1763, Charles Cessna Sr applied for a Warrant of 100 acres in Cumberland County. Land was next to John Cessna Jr, known by the name of the Block Houses. Warrant cost £9. Annual Quit Rents were 4sh 2p.

On 23 November 1766 James Levingston sold 100 acres to Charles Cessna (Sr). Land near the block houses.

On 14July 1774, David Jennings sold 100 acres to Charles Cessna (Jr.)

In 1783, Col. Charles Cessna (Jr) was prosecuted for forgery during his service as County Commissioner. As a result, the following ad appeared in the paper.

29 Mar 1786, Sale of Plantation and late property of Charles Ceffna esq, in Cumberland Valley, on Great Road from Bedford to Cumberland. 300 acres: apply to Thomas Coulter, esq near premises; George Funk in Bedford, or Thos Smith, James Hamilton, or Thos Duncan in Carlisle. Abstracts from Carlisle Gazette:

(Notes in PA Archives list Hamilton and Duncan applying to the government for reimbursement of their services in selling this land).

In the Fall of 1783, Col. Charles and family moved homestead new lands in Georgia. At the same time, his brother Evan moved to Pittsburg.

THE INDICATION IS: That at the beginning of an Indian War, when people are fleeing Western Pennsylvania, the Cessnas were investing. John Cessna (son of the Frenchman and born in Ireland) purchases four separate farms of 300 acres each, for the Warrant Price of £27 each. The originals of these warrants indicate the names of people who have already made improvements on them. It would seem that as people fled, John Cessna purchased Quit Claims from them, then went to the Land Office in Carlisle and applied for his own Warrants.

Evan, Jonathan & Joseph were all underage. Robert Hall and Thomas Jones were his sons-in-law.

Charles Cessna Sr. purchased a 100-acre farm, in June, a month after John made his purchases. It appears that he occupied his farm soon after, and in the coming years added two more 100-acre farms to his.